# Katrina: When God Closed His Eyes on New Orleans

Tyierra R. Henderson

*For every motherless child*
*That was always told that they couldn't...*
*But still did.*

*"The best way to not feel hopeless is to get up and do something. Don't wait for good things to happen to you. If you go out and make some good things happen, you will fill the world with hope, you will fill yourself with hope."*

**- Barack Obama**

# To All the Opinionated Disbelievers...

On any other occasion I wouldn't do this. I would not amuse those who are here strictly for my entertainment, but I will today. I believe we all deserve a tiny bit of notice every now and again and these few words are for you and the "you" I refer to already know who you are.

Before you read these pages of my life and dare push your nose up at who I was, who I am now, or who I dream to become ask yourself: Was I there? Look at yourself in the mirror and be completely honest, something most of those who seek for me to hurt may fear, and really think of how you made this situation, my situation, or anyone's situation outside your own, better. Were you there? If you can't say you were or that you tried, if you can't help the situation or say anything positive, then don't "say" at all.

Just listen, read, grow, and learn. Hopefully my story can help you find yours. I hope that once you finish, once you close the back cover and the last sentence is completed, you will understand me and who I am. With any luck, the way you have viewed me and so blindly judged others in the past without knowing what lies beneath the surface will change. I do not want to continue the cycle of hatred that has been viciously destroying the love that we should have for one another. I want to start a new dream where we all are in this together because we never know how many more people may be living a life far worse than our own. WE have work to do.

# Acknowledgments

My story is not my story alone. If it were not for the voices, support, and motivation from others this book would still be a work in progress. If I could I'd have everyone, including the negative people I have unfortunately dealt with, who have contributed to the success of my story highlighted but my pen only has so much ink. Because of this I will speak only on the few people who have greatly impacted my life in a positive way and gotten me to this point.

To my grandparents, please understand that I love you dearly and you did more for me than most would. Because of what you tried to do for me I am who I am today. You taught me more than you think you did. I learned how bad it could be but furthermore how strong I am. I also learned how to survive and make a way out of no way. You are my heart and I love you no matter what. Now just answer the phone when I call!

To my uncle, Burnell, who has always been more like a brother than anything to me. I thank you for doing what you could. In no way did I expect you to do everything. You were in the same boat I was in. I thank you for being you. And thank you again for my lettermen jacket.

To Shandrika, my ace, you have been with me from the very beginning and through all my ups and downs. You listened to my cries and you didn't tell everyone at school about those roaches that ran across the floor when you visited. I want to thank you for not judging me because of how I looked and for wanting to take the time to understand my story. You have always been a genuine friend to me even to this day.

To Terrian, my sweet lady, you are my inspiration. When I finally grow up, I want to be just like you. Going from the afterthought to the head of the line. You are the poster child for success and I am so proud of you! If no one else is, trust me I am! And now that you are a fancy chef, I expect cheesecake and crawfish Étouffée on a regular. Keep pushing no matter what they say!

To all of my sisters, I love you and I always wanted to be a great big sister. I just wanted to give you all something to look up to. I know we did not grow up side by side but that doesn't mean we aren't family. I will always be your big sister and I can't wait for the day we have our girl's trip.

To Sheena, my love, you are an amazing woman and you make me better. Without you I would still be accepting less than what I am worth. You gave me the knowledge that other women didn't give to me. You helped me on my road to discovering myself. You make our family whole. Without your inspiration and creativeness, this story would have never been completed or even had a finished cover. Thank you! You are my motivation and I love you!

To my baby boy Ja'Mauri. Mommy has done all she could to make sure you never went without. I know in this moment you may not understand why I work as hard as I do but one day you will. You were part of the motivation for me to keep pushing and for me to share my story. I love you always.

Last, Yolanda, my birth mother, I thank you. You taught me more in your absence than you ever would even if you were sitting in the seat right next to me. You of all of those above know the least about the true story of Tyierra but you make up the greatest amount of it. I hope each page helps you find not only who your daughter has become but what type of mother you truly are.

# "The Bulletin"

National Weather Service

New Orleans LA

1011AM CDT Sun Aug 28 2005

*...Devastating Damage Expected...*

Hurricane Katrina...a most powerful hurricane with unprecedented strength...rivaling the intensity of Hurricane Camille of 1969.

Most of the area will be uninhabitable for weeks...perhaps longer. At least one half of well-constructed homes will have roof and wall failure. All gabled roofs will fail...leaving those homes severely damaged or destroyed.

The majority of industrial buildings will become nonfunctional. Partial to complete wall and roof failure is expected. All wood framed low rising apartment buildings will be destroyed. Concrete block low rise apartments will sustain major damage...including some wall and roof failure.

High rise office and apartment buildings will sway dangerously...a few to the point of total collapse. All windows will blow out.

Airborne debris will be widespread...and may include heavy items such as household appliances and even light vehicles. Sport utility vehicles and light trucks will be moved. The blow debris will create additional destruction. Persons...pets...and livestock exposed to the winds will face certain death if struck.

Power outages will last for weeks...as most power poles will be down and transformers destroyed. Water shortages will make human suffering incredible by modern standards.

The vast majority of native trees will be snapped or uprooted. Only the heartiest will remain standing...but be totally defoliated. Few crops will remain. Livestock left exposed to the winds will be killed.

An inland hurricane wind warning is issued when sustained winds near hurricane force...or frequent gusts at or above hurricane force...are certain within the next 12 to 24 hours.

# Chapter 1: An Uncle's Greed

*"The only two things you can truly depend upon are gravity and greed."*

**-Jack Palance**

The sun was already up and sneaking into my window early on Sunday August 28, 2005. My 65-year-old grandpa, who was really my step-grandfather if there is such a thing, walked into the room and pulled the covers from my body.

"Get up, girl!" his deep voice yelled, "and make some pancakes for me and your grandma." He was standing there, shirtless as usual, waiting for my reaction. His brown belt was not buckled and his pants sagged a little revealing his plaid boxers. His chocolate skin was smooth minus that covering his knuckles.

I slapped my beaten pillow on top of my head. "I'm still sleeping," my raspy voice cracked, "it's too early."

"I'll make you a deal. If you can guess what time it is, I'll let you sleep in a little longer. If not, you got to get your tail up. We not raising a bum," I knew this was a trick as it always was with his deals but I thought I had no other options. I knew we only had enough mix for a couple pancakes and that was if the bugs hadn't got to it first and I would rather rest than get up and get half a flapjack.

There was an old brown clock that my grandpa had gotten from a thrift store about a month before on the side of my bed that he didn't know I could see. I quickly glanced over to see the time. "Eight seventeen?" I said trying not to sound too dishonest.

My grandfather paused before snatching the cooled pillow from my face, "Too, bad! Get up anyway and make some breakfast." He walked out of the room I shared with my already awaken grandmother and plopped in his favorite seat on the sofa.

I pulled myself to my feet, angry and drowsy. I dragged from the bed to the bathroom to wash my face and brush my teeth. Soon, I found myself walking into the kitchen to begin cooking the pancakes my grandfather so desperately wanted. It was just something about not letting me sleep during the weekend that my grandfather must have enjoyed. Maybe he was trying to teach me a lesson of some sort, but I didn't get it. No sleeping in and no naps. At the time I felt my grandfather, Burnell Harris Sr., was just a mean old grumpy man.

I never really knew how he felt. I couldn't tell if he was proud of me, disappointed, or somewhere in the middle. He really was an emotionless man outside of anger. For a long time, the words "I love you" formed in a sentence, didn't exist to him. Grandpa Burnell was more of a James Evans from Good Times than a Cliff Huxtable from The Cosby Show. I knew he cared because he was there, but then again I wouldn't bet money on it. He had a bad limp in his left leg that made him look like he was wobbling back and forth everywhere he went. He told me the story of him getting bit by a snake which caused that noticeable hobbling a million times but I never believed it. He was king of half-truths and whole lies.

My grandfather wasn't related to me by blood, but he had taken me under his wing when I was just a few weeks old while in a relationship with maternal grandmother. He took me in after my then 17-year-old mother, Yolanda, ran off. They were all I had. This left me to refer to my grandparents for parental guidance which, depending on the day, wasn't the best.

The three of us, my grandparents and I, lived in a one-bedroom apartment in the New Orleans East. We hadn't been there for more than three months by that late August. My grandma and grandpa never owned anything and we never stayed at one residence for more than a year or so, if that. Grandpa Burnell had a thing for not paying bills. From time to time, the landlord would have pity on him because he had a "little girl" and didn't want to put me out on the street. That didn't always happen but I had grown use to that life.

I fixed two pancakes; one for my grandpa and one for me. We chased the sweet morning cake down with a side of the last two eggs in the fridge. My grandma didn't eat as she claimed to have stomach pains and really was not hungry. When there wasn't enough to go around she would sometime make excuses not to eat so I could get a bigger share. She just sat on the couch and waited for the two of us to finish our meal while reading her Bible and humming a church hymn.

My grandma, Ludie Oliphant, was a Bible thumper if you ever did meet one. No one goes by every word in the good book but she sure did know what it said. It drove my grandad crazy to hear her up at two in the morning banging a kid's piano screaming, or singing as she calls it, at the top of her lungs about how she's been running for the Lord and her feet ain't tired yet. She just could not be stopped once she got going. Grandma Ludie was a beautiful woman. Her skin was fair and her hair long and black. She attracted a lot of eyes when we went out, but she was a "holy woman" and wasn't going to be swept up in the clutches of Satan.

After breakfast, I went and sat on the bed that I wished I was sleeping in. My grandmother's side was not made up from when she had gotten up earlier. I addressed the green covers before pulling out some paper to write on. I looked around my room for inspiration. It wasn't much to be inspired by besides a large poster of Bow Wow tapped to the back of my closet door. I loved to write. I wanted to grow up to be an investigational reporter and I just knew that one day I would work behind some anchor desk somewhere like CNN. However, in that day I had no words to write. I just sat there blank for a while before I heard my grandfather's voice.

It was nearly ten o'clock when my grumpy grandad called me into the living room. I thought it was for me to finish cleaning the kitchen that I had destroyed. I was going to clean it soon enough. I was hoping to write but maybe sneak in a nap before he noticed I was gone. He told me to take a seat next to my grandma to watch the news. Something big was about to happen.

We sat in an anxious wait for the New Orleans Mayor Clarence Nagin Jr., commonly known as Ray Nagin, to appear on the tiny TV screen. A hurricane was speeding in our direction and we were unsure if we should stay and ride the wave or hit the road. The faith of the Big Easy's residents rested on Mr. Nagin's next words. We had already been told that we would not be going to school that next day because of the storm but we didn't know what to expect.

I glanced over at the window and saw the sun was still slightly poking through. There weren't any real signs of a storm. It wasn't unusual to see a threat of a hurricane in late August in New Orleans. But I, nor anyone I knew, took hurricanes seriously. Hurricanes didn't ever hit New Orleans. They may have looked as if they were coming our way, but they always managed to swerve or die down before making land fall. To us, it was just a day off of school, maybe some rain and a little wind, but outside of about maybe three inches of flood water nothing really happened. When I turned back from the raggedy blinds, seeing the look on my grandfather face and the warnings from the TV even before the appearance of our city's leader I knew this was not like before. Sitting there, and looking at the screen, this was different. This was not what we were used to.

The Mayor finally walked on to the screen. I remember a few seconds of dead silence come over both my house and where the press conference was being held. We were about to witness the beginning of a historic event. Mr. Nagin's words undoubtable changed everything I had ever knew. The warning that dripped from his lips told the ears that listened that New Orleans was under its first ever mandatory evacuation. My eyes began to water, my teeth started to tremble, and I just felt my life was about to change.

"I want to emphasize, the first choice of every citizen should be to leave the city," The mayor stole a look at the faces in the room. You could hear it in his voice and see the sternness in his face. This was not a cry for attention. This was really happening and I didn't even know what it actually meant. I didn't know how to truly feel because this had never happened before.

Every time a hurricane would breeze past Louisiana, thousands of people would pack up their minivans and hit the freeway. Because of heat exhaustion and backed up interstates a lot of those who left didn't always make it back. I can still remember how soft the leaves blew down our empty street from the hurricane that was going to break all records, but never did just the year before. Instead we got a drizzle and a day at home with no class.

"Call Juney!" my grandfather instructed me. His eyes never left the television screen. He wanted to process as much information as he possibly could. He was scared, something I had never seen in him before.

I picked up the house phone and rang my uncle, Burnell Jr., who was a driver for King Cab at the time. My uncle was more of a brother then anything. His cute baby face always attracted attention from the city's women folk. His smile was packed with the New Orleans tradition of gold teeth, something he got as soon as he graduated from high school. He was the youngest of the three children my grandmother had and the only child she had with Grandpa Burnell.

When he finally answered, I told him the awful news. He had already heard parts of it from others who had called to locate him for services. He asked to speak with his father. I handed the phone over to my grandpa so that the two of them could come up with a plan. Just like more than 110,000 other residents of New Orleans, we didn't have a car. I can't even remember the last time I saw either of my grandparents behind a steering wheel. Juney would be our only hope out of the city.

"Alright," my grandpa whispered as he hung up the phone after a plot driven call, "he said he is going to come pick us up in a little bit and we'll all drive to Alexandria to Bessie-Mae's house. So you two can go ahead and pack the stuff you need."

My grandmother stood up and gazed at her partner for a while as if she was observing him for a true reaction. He did not look at her probably in fear of terrifying the two of us. My grandad tried to stay calm but my grandma could still sense the fear. We never left during a storm because Grandpa Burnell wasn't afraid of anything. He was made of steel. This time it was different. Now we had no other choice but to go see his sister, Bessie-Mae, for safety.

Into the bedroom I went to begin packing as I was told. I grabbed a few shirts, a pair of earrings, two pairs of jeans, and a handful of menstrual pads.

I rushed to grab my toothbrush. After throwing them into my bag, I took a quick glance around my room.

What am I missing? Oh my goodness! I need underwear!

I sprinted through the top drawer of my dresser and grabbed about a weeks' worth of undies and threw them on top of the other unorganized and unfolded items in the bag. I took another look around and there was my flower and glitter covered poem book sitting at the bottom of my underwear draw. I took it into my hands, looked it once over, and stuffed it on the side of my sack. I didn't need my grandad to see that at all.

My grandmother suggested we pack some food and water for the drive but my grandfather suggested against it. My Aunt Bessie-Mae gave us tons of food with every visit. Her house was small but her property was quite large. There were huge trees and soft green grass. And the pecans! They covered her fenced in yard. I would spend hours walking in circles picking up pecans to crack open on her front porch. But this time, the drive to Alexandria was going to be different.

We got dressed to be ready for when my uncle arrived but my grandmother felt something was wrong. After getting dressed, she stayed in the backroom and hugged her Bible.

"Where is that boy?" She sat on the edge of the bed in wonder. It was almost half past eleven when the worry started to really set into my grandma. She wanted to know where her son was and what was keeping him. My grandma wanted frantically to call him and just check in on his well-being, then again she didn't want to bother him either. Her worry was clearly visible. I left her with her thoughts to sit in the living room and wait.

My grandfather sat in a wobbly leg chair he placed in front of the TV. He was dressed wearing his worn work shoes and one of the few stripped collared shirts he had. A couple others he had instructed me to pack in my bag along with a pair of khaki pants. His old hands were tangled with one another as he sat waiting for more news and the arrival of his son. But the arrival would never come.

The phone finally rang. I handed it over to my grandfather so he could speak with my nervous voiced uncle.

"What!?" my grandpa yelled into the receiver as he tried to get a better grip. It was nearing one in the afternoon when my uncle called us to tell us he wasn't coming. Juney had left the city limits to drop a young lady in Baton Rouge who paid him $200 cash for his efforts, but now he couldn't get back in the city. My uncle's greed had cost his family a way to safety and possibly our lives. We were stuck with no way out.

"You're not worth nothing! That's why I don't get on this damn phone and talk to you! You make me sick! How could you leave us here? You're a selfish man!" he threw the phone against the wall and both my grandmother and I jumped from fear. The phone broke into several pieces as it landed on the floor but we dared not look at my grandpa in the eyes. We found a spot of the floor and kept our heads down. Luckily my grandmother had a prepaid cell phone for me to carry. She tried to call my uncle on the cheap device but had no luck. We were on our own.

Then hope came across the TV that still played faintly in the background. My grandfather increased the volume of the television. Words spilled into our ears that for those that could not get out of the city we were welcomed to ride the storm out in the Superdome. It was our only option. We had no other choice but to take it.

Without hesitation or permission my grandmother rushed to the kitchen. She placed one of our rusty black pots in the sink to fill it with water. She started to boil hot dog wieners for us to have something to eat. Her hands were shaking as she brought the pot to the burner. We had to have something to eat if we were going to be stuck in the Superdome.

My grandma and I telepathically agreed to stay clear of my grandfather for a while. He needed to cool down. While I was trying to find spare Wal-Mart bags to put our hot dogs into my grandfather shared the plan he had been thinking up in his head.

"Look...we are going to have to walk down to Abramson High School and catch that bus down to the dome before that storm comes," he leaned back in his wooden chair he had bought not even a week before from a nearby thrift store. "So y'all women need to hurry up!"

While we prepared the last bit of food we had, which wasn't much because it was the end of the month, my grandad began to explain why the dome was about to be a temporary home. Juney had left the city with his passenger and headed out to the state capital to ensure the security of her life. When he turned around and tried to reenter the city, he was not allowed to. He was turned around and told to keep it moving. It made no sense to allow someone to drive into the pits of hell. Now his entire family was stuck in the city. A city that is well known to be below sea level. Stuck in a city where one of the biggest storms in history strolls towards it.

It wasn't a new thing to see my grandad's face as he frowned at my grandmother. She was prancing around the house like a mad woman yelling that "this was the devils work." God apparently was going to let this evil happen to clean up shop in the Big Easy and clear out all the sin. She just did not understand how annoying she could be sometimes. My grandad tried to ignore her by getting ready to leave. He turned off his TV, tucked away his Bible and opened the door. We had a long walk ahead of us.

The sun was out high and hot and had pushed out the gray clouds, as most summer days in New Orleans that morning. I couldn't help but feel bad for my grandad. His bad knee was giving him issues as we scattered along. The walk was more than two miles and there we were, not even five minutes out the door, and we all had already broken a sweat. A breeze would walk by every now and again but nothing to brag about. I was afraid that neither one of them would make it. My grandad had just turned 65 and my grandma was 53.

I had way too much on my mind to worry for all three of us. I was dragging a huge red suitcase behind me. I still can hear the wheels jumping around on the concrete. It was real work pulling that bag. As we walked past the bus stop where I caught the bus towards uptown every day, I had to stop to catch up with my thoughts. I took a long look back. Would I see that street the same way? My grandma saw how far I was and yelled for me to put some pep in my step. I closed my hands around the handle of my roller luggage and started up again.

The walk to the high school was quite long. We thought we would be able to stop and get some snacks for the trip at one of the few stores we had to walk by on our way there but all of them were closed. At the last store, Walgreens, my grandfather stood and stared at the automatic doors as if he was waiting for them to magically open. The look on his face told me he felt helpless. He could not keep us safe. He could not do anything.

In the parking lot of Abramson High, the same high school my uncle graduated from years before, there was a city bus already there and being loaded. My excitement level peaked seeing the New Orleans RTA sitting there waiting on passengers and knowing I would no longer have to face the heat. My dream was soon shattered when the driver told the remaining citizens that the bus was at capacity. We were told to hold on and wait for the next bus to arrive.

Countless boxes, suitcases and backpacks lined the sidewalk. Many of us had packed our whole lives in one carry-on luggage. Most only packed a few days of clothes thinking that soon we would be returning. While others did not want to leave anything behind.

During the wait I called a few friends to check on them and their safety. The last was my good friend Terrian Marchand. We went to the same school and spent most of our time together on the phone. I wanted to see if she and her family were okay before the storm came. I knew cell reception was going to flat line sooner or later as it often did in hurricanes. I really wanted to see if they were going to the dome, too. I figured if she and her family did I would have someone to talk to and to go into this storm with.

"We're fine," Terrian said to me, "and I don't think we're going anywhere. We should be safe here. We live in the projects girl! Nothing can move these things!" Terrian and her family lived in one of the most structurally sound buildings in the city that could probably withstand anything. We said our good-byes and told each other to be safe before ending the call.

Another bus pulled up minutes after arriving, but it seemed more like hours. The three of us were able to board this convey. Others who arrived after us weren't as fortunate. It took a good thirty minutes to load the whole bus before we pulled off. I looked out the window as our ride's engine began to hum. I watched as the roads passed us by and noticed that the streets had become deserted. There were no kids playing and no families to be seen on their way home from church. The stillness of the streets made them seem like photographs.

I became a little nervous when the bus entered the freeway. All the traffic was at a standstill in one direction and we were going the opposite way. My thoughts began to run around in my mind. What if we run right into the storm? I shook off the wicked feelings. We will be fine. Even my greedy uncle. I took a deep breath and told myself I was going to be alright over and over again until we reached the dome. When I stepped off the bus, suitcase in hand, something told me things would never be the same. Only thing running through my mind was how my uncle could allow his greed to come before his family, leaving us trapped in the path of Katrina.

# Chapter 2: Bus Stop Battles

*"Lots of people want to ride with you in the limo, but what you want is someone who will take the bus with you when the limo breaks down."*
**-Oprah Winfrey**

Riding that bus to the Superdome that Sunday brought me back to every time I sat on that faithful RTA, also known as the Regional Transit Authority. My family didn't have enough money for a car, so we practically rode that thing everywhere. From church, to school, to work, and even to the grocery store. If only I had a quarter for the many days I carried almost $250 worth of Winn-Dixie groceries all the way home using only my hands and the public bus.

It wasn't unusual or uncommon for the people from my community to not own cars or even know how to drive for that matter. Despite having the RTA, I think that maybe the real reason was due to their lack of credit and willingness to better themselves. Then again, it's a strong possibility it was because they just never had the opportunity or chance. Cars just were not affordable for a lot of us Louisianans and no one had time or cared to learn how to drive. I guess we all felt that knowing how to drive was a privilege more than an actual necessity.

I took two buses to get to my school, McMain, from home every day while still living uptown on Louisiana Avenue Parkway; the Napoleon and South Claiborne. I considered school my time away from my grandparents. I would ride the bus with a few of my classmates, and it kind of made me feel like I was a normal child like everyone else around me even if I was just sitting and waiting to pull the cord to make my exit. That was not a feeling I sensed often. The low growl of the bus as it carried me to my destination sometimes put me to sleep, it was my white noise. I would just be so comfortable in those hard-plastic seats; it was my second home. As long as I gave my ticket to the mouth of the bus, I was invited to take a seat and enjoy the ride every day. That was the only thing I knew I could rely on. It may have been late or packed but it was always there for me. It was my time away from those I called family but it didn't last long. Once we moved further away from my school, both of my grandparents began riding right next to me.

The bus was a lot of things for me, but safe was not one of them. I have seen some very peculiar things happen on the ghetto limo as I call it. With New Orleans being a party town, the area had its ups and downs. There have been moments where I've seen people blatantly drunk waddling up the steps of the bus in the middle of the day. I have seen people take off their hair, throw trash at others, and untrained kids grabbing others bags and shoes and taking off as the bus doors opens. Saturday morning cartoons had nothing on a long ride on the RTA but those were the battles of the bus.

Then there were the battles at the bus stops as we waited. School aged boys and sometime girls would all circle up around the purple, gold, and green signs and have rap clashes. Someone drops a beat on a hardcover textbook with a couple of number two pencils while others would start beatboxing. It was different and they weren't as bad as you would imagine an 8th grader would be. The battles I witnessed could be easily thrown into movies like 8 Mile. The talented kids in those battles were untouchable. I guess it can be expected in a city that raised people like Lil' Wayne, Mannie Fresh, Mystikal, Birdman, and Master P. The little concerts would keep my mind off the wait. It was a great experience and I loved to bounce my head to the beat.

There were also the random encounters between couples. Often you can see these new relationships blooming. Young people would openly kiss and hold hands. Some girls would even sit on their cute boyfriend's lap when there weren't any seats left in a packed bus until the driver told them to get off in the name of safety. If only their parents knew where their hands had been while sitting in the loveseats in the back of the bus on their ride home. While that was middle and high school puppy love, there was also the hardcore down and dirty love; the love you would fight for.

A tiny young woman wearing a ponytail, no older than twenty-five, sat in the bus's double seats in front of me. She seemed to be in deep thought as she stared out the window with her big brown eyes that I could see reflecting in the window of the bus. Signs of being tired and worn down filled the atmosphere around her. The woman's light skin revealed the dark bags under her eyes with ease. I can recall her chewing on a piece of pink bubble gum really loud, forcing small pops over and over. It was clear it was getting annoying when the driver glanced back in the rear view mirror. Others tried to ignore the sound of her chewing the gum but it was impossible.

We were on the Martin L. King bus headed towards what was known as the Calliope Housing Projects in the third ward of the city. The bus was calm when the young lady in front of me began to ruffle through her bag. It was her cell phone ringing. The young lady pulled the big black brick out of her purse and answered.

"Hello?" Her accent clearly showed signs she had been living in New Orleans her whole life, "Yea I'm on my way to the house now. What's up, woe? HE WHAT?! He got WHO in my house!?!"

The riders and I instantly fixed our eyes in her direction. The words out of her mouth could have made a sinner blush. A friend of hers had seen her boyfriend brining a young lady in the building where they lived that the friend did not recognize. After another couple of minutes of her trying to figure out who this female was that was apparently "sitting on her couch and drinking her juice" she hung up the phone. The petite lady started bouncing around in her seat and shaking her head.

"This dude thinks it's a game? He done did this mess too many times! I'm 'bout to go to jail!" the young lady spoke out loud directing none of the words to anyone in particular but probably in hopes someone would agree. Some of the people on the bus tried to ignore her while others couldn't help but glance back at the toddler fit she was throwing.

The rage in her eyes frightened some of the passengers. As the bus continued to move, the angry woman stood to begin making her way to the door. She paced back and forth, swinging her ponytail as she moved. You can tell she was thinking hard on how she was going to murder her boyfriend. The bus finally got close to her stop. She pulled the cord rapidly over and over to alert the driver it was time for her departure. As she continued to think out loud, she removed her shoes. She jumped a little in place and shook her head the same as a boxer would before entering the ring.

The bus slowed and finally opened the rear doors. She broke through the double exits and off she went in a full sprint towards trouble down the street. The bus stayed parked until she disappeared behind one of the giant dirty red brick buildings that made up the Calliope. I never saw her again. I still wonder sometimes what her rage led to.

There is one instance on a bus stop that I still question. It was during my 7th grade year, a couple boys were hanging at the bus stop waiting for their ride to arrive. I was standing nearby with a classmate. School had just let out and we all were ready to head home. The unfamiliar faces seemed to be going about their normal day. I overheard them talking about some of the girls they went to school with and what they were going to do after getting out of their uniforms. Both were clearly older and possibly a grade higher. The first was light skinned with a pretty smile. The other had a darker complexion and sported a set of braces. Neither of them went to the school I did.

A few buses had already passed but didn't stop because they were filled to capacity. I didn't mind the wait because all I thought was how it was just more time I can get to myself before going home. It was a nice day, hot as usual, but there were a few trees to protect us and a small breeze we would get from passing cars. The intersection was filled with noise from loud turning trucks and people blowing their horns.

It wasn't long before a group of five older guys began to cross the street in our direction. It was easy to see they hadn't been to school that day with the absence of their uniforms. Two of them had removed their school shirts in which they were draping over their shoulders. The clothes they did wear were baggy and barely holding up.

One of them had short dreads that he was attempting to grow. He twisted a few as he strolled across the street. Another had a well groomed beard and was using the brush he used to tame the hair on his head to also calm the hairs on his face. The others went simple and had low cut fades. All of them seemed up to no good.

As they approached, they gave my friend and I a sour look but said nothing. Both of us looked towards the ground to avoid eye contact. As they passed us, they "greeted" the two boys who shared the stop. The boys who were originally at the stop looked down at the ground and refused to say anything back.

"Lil' boy! You don't hear him talking to yo ol' stank ass?" the young boy who sported dreads pressed his body against the fair skinned kid after not receiving the salutations he thought the group deserved.

"What? You think you better than somebody? You got your prep boy shirt on and you think you better than us? When somebody speak to you, you speak back! I know your mama taught you better than that!" The boy's body heat was surly making his victim uncomfortable. The bully's friend he was defending seemed uninterested in what was going on but the remainder of the group snickered as they watched. They knew this was all a game.

The aggressor continued his nudging and the target tried with all his might to ignore the violence that he was facing. "Don't be a punk bitch!" The bully continued to taunt him as he spoke cruelly, "First you don't speak just like a punk, now you gone let me just push you around like one of my girls? We don't do well with pretty boys around here!" The tall, slender African American boy would not let up on the prey. He continued to badger him, the pushing and shoving got even harder and there was no sign of the bus.

The fair-skinned boy seemed to be getting aggravated with the assault on his little body, "Man, move!" he jerked his shoulder away from him attempting to hold on to his backpack as it was slipping down his arm, "Y'all ain't got nothing else to do?" The boy spoke without looking at anyone specific.

"Yea," the lead bully looked back at his friends as he smirked, "But I'ma mess with you first." The ramming of his finger into the quite boy's body continued while the group laughed. The picking just wouldn't stop. The group of bullies pulled his shirt, dragged his bag from his back, and called him a number of rude names. It got so violent the boy began to shed tears. He tried to maintain his manliness with the anger in his face but it was not easy. It was noticeable in his eyes that he was hurt. His friend couldn't do anything but standby and pray he wasn't next. He knew these guys would start on him the second he unlocked his lips to impede on the violence. He just backed up and watched the outcome.

"Man, I said stop!" He raised his voice at the street corner tyrant in hopes of scaring him away.

"Or what?" He dared also rising the base of his voice.

The little boy was fed up. He dropped his bag filled with the books and notes of the day. His small fist danced at his waist. His head was slightly tilted to the side as he stared his opponent in the face. His eyebrows wrinkled up and his eyes were still watered. He took in deep breaths, one after another. He was going to resolve this bully issue once and for all.

"I said or what? You think you scaring somebody? What you gonna..." Before the tough guy could get another word out of his mouth the small and irritated kid he was just poking at had turned into a man. The victim had taken his fist, pulled it back and with the speed of a slingshot slammed it into the left side of the oppressor's face. You could see the rest of his sentence dripping from his lip.

The situation was not made any better after that when his friends began to laugh at him. My classmate and I just stood there in dismay. It was unbelievable how hard he had hit the much taller and stronger boy. The kid who was being picked on couldn't believe what he did either. His friend's face read disbelief. They both quickly went from skepticism to fear knowing what that two seconds of victory was without a doubt about to lead to. Surprisingly, the friends of the teaser continued cracking up. They pointed and called him countless cheeky names to emasculate his ego.

"SHUT THE HELL UP!" he yelled to his friends. He jammed his mug shot into the fearful boy's face and then repaid him with an equally damaging punch to the face. The hit was so hard the light skinned boy fell back on his hands. The dread head began to beat and slap the now crying middle schooler on the ground. The little guy attempted to fight back, but it was useless. The brute strength that held him down was too much. He beat, slapped, and kicked the now crying student. Cars just drove by ignoring what was happening. The beating went on for a good while before an older member of the five-boy pack decided it was enough.

"Alright, alright," the guy with the full beard said in a deep voice, "that's enough, man. Let him go." He walked over to them and pulled them apart. The kid was shoved once more ending up back on the ground as he tripped on his own shoe that had come off during the scuffle. The crowd departed from the bus stop and off to devastate the lives of other innocent people.

The other boy picked his friend's backpack from the sidewalk and handed it to him as he began standing once more. The darker brace face boy asked his friend if he was okay. The injured boy nodded trying to avoid showing his face was still damp from the tears. He had a few scratches above his eye and his cheek was already beginning to swell. Some blood had dripped to his school shirt. Besides the surface, and his pride, he had made it through.

The bus finally arrived. When we jumped on, I was a little relieved. The bus driver and the other passengers had no look of concern on their faces. I guess seeing a middle school student with a bloody uniform shirt was normal business for them. We were all, in a sense, safe from what had just happened. It was over and though his face hurt a little, he would live to fight another day.

That was the only beauty I could actually see about the entire situation and majority of the fights in New Orleans at the time. While there may have been a little sprinkle of blood every now and again, the confrontations never escalated to gun violence. A mean right hook and a few harsh words being passed was all it took.

I could tell tears wanted to escape his eyes, but much like other boys in the Big Easy, he had to pretend to be a man, he had to be strong. While he may have not won that fight, he had mentally grown and knew what to do next time. New Orleans was not a place associated with how many books you read but instead how many battles you won. He definitely earned his ride home on the RTA that day.

# Chapter 3: "Let Us In!"

*"Let the rain kiss you. Let the rain beat upon your head with silver liquid drops. Let the rain sing you a lullaby."*
**-Langston Hughes**

We took a look toward the entrance of the dome and saw what seemed like most of New Orleans standing in line in front of us. My grandfather's eyes grew big as he scanned the crowd. He just knew the bus was going to pull up to the entrance door and we would be able to stroll right in without any problems.

We stood there in line and waited for what seemed like hours. There was nothing for us to do but stand or sit on our luggage and wait. My grandmother hummed a spiritual tune while my grandpa picked at his hand in deep thought. There was nothing but opportunity for us to think. I can remember thinking about what I was going to do when I got back to school in a couple of days.

It was the beginning of the school year but I already had plans to make it a year to remember. It was my freshman year in high school and I was finally about to be something. I was going to take my high school days to transform, I was going to bloom. I was always the ugly duckling in my own mind and a lot of people from grade school would agree. I was taller than everyone around me and the brightest, too. I was a stick and you could see my ribs when I pulled up my shirt. My hair was a bright sandy red and goldish color which was never combed. My grandmother didn't know how to do my hair so I found myself often pulling it back into a messy ponytail. I was that girl, the one who just stuck out.

That was all over now, I just knew my freshman year was going to be it! I was going to go to my first football game, my first dance, and maybe experience my first real love even if my grandfather would hate it. I was going to figure it out, I had hopes this would be my year.

The sun was beginning to disappear and it started to cool. Looking at all the faces standing in wait, for a split second I was reminded of a normal lazy afternoon. The only things we were missing was a bucket full of crawfish from Cajun's Seafood on Broad and Washington and a pineapple Big Shot soda.

There were kids of all ages running around playing tag. You could see the joy in their faces knowing there would be no school in the morning. Parents were so distracted with the lack of cell phone service to notice that children were sprinting in small circles to busy themselves. I tried to call my uncle a couple of times to see where he could be and if he was doing okay but his phone went right to voicemail.

When my grandparents weren't looking I tried to ring my mother, Yolanda, who lived a few hours away in Georgia at the time but I got no answer. I knew she had already heard of what was going on in New Orleans and wondered why she hadn't tried to contact me. I was afraid she would never reach out to me again. I feared I was going to start high school, another milestone in my life, without her. I just really wanted her to answer.

I wanted her to know that I was okay and how I deeply yearned for the opportunity to meet my younger sisters. I was tired of being alone in this world. Although my family is big, I knew only very few of them. My granddad did not like to keep in contact with family. I think it was mostly because he wasn't proud of how we had to live sometimes. Distant cousins and great aunts would ask my grandmother if they could vacation in the Crescent City all the time when I was young, but they were told no so much that at some point they just gave up asking. There was only one occasion I can remember where my grandmother actually tried to get them to visit and she failed. Grandma Ludie told her sister to drive from Texas to New Orleans but didn't tell her partner. When they arrived, my grandpa stood behind the door and did not allow them to enter. My grandma and I just sat there on the floor not allowed to speak until they left.

I didn't have cousins around my age. My mother had me so young that no one had a chance to have children to provide me playmates. My Uncle Juney was the closest person I had to a friend and brother than anyone else, even with the twelve years between us. I was proud to tell people that I was his sister and he was my brother. Even when he use to beat me up during commercial breaks of his favorite shows, The Jerry Springer Show and Maury. I didn't even mind when he locked me in his closet, he was literally all the happiness I had sometimes. He made my childhood bearable. As I thought of him not answering, I felt my eyes begin to water. I missed him.

"New Orleans don't know what they doing," one lady said interrupting my thoughts. She stood there speaking her mind while rocking a hair wrap that was falling down in the back.

"Why they trying to get the whole city to evacuate hours before? We all could be dead!" asked a middle aged man sitting on the ground.

"Lord, it's gone be problems in here! I can feel it!" explained another woman behind me, "You can't put this many black folks in the same place without something going wrong."

People around silently agreed by nodding their heads up and down. Others stated it would only be for a couple days and we would be back home in no time. My grandma tried to talk to others around us and express how she emphasized with them but my grandfather quickly reminded her that we were not in a place to start making friends.

Looking around, it was a sea of African American faces. I thought of the Superdome as our modern day Noah's Arc but maybe it wasn't. Maybe it was the Jesus of Lubeck, a German ship given to Sir John Hawkins by Queen Elizabeth that was to transport African people to the Americans. This was to be done only if the people chose to go. If they did not want to they were not to be forced. Sir Hawkins promised the African men, women, and children free land and hopes on the other end of the ship's voyage, much like what we were being promised. Those people, of free mind and spirit were in search for sanctuary, prosperity, and happiness but found themselves the property of man. Would we too be the same?

As we stood there on Sugar Bowl Drive a number of vans began to pull up with camera crews swiftly sliding the long automobile doors open. A few from the local news were also out to document this page of New

Orleans history, others were from the Weather Channel. They felt obligated to come out to see what had formed in front of the famous arena and was determined to get the not so valued opinions of the city's citizens.

The teams flipped on their cameras and began to pan the crowd. Some timidly turned away and pretended the cameras were not there by covering their faces. Others decided this was a good time to let the world know how much they disagreed with the decisions that had been made.

"Do you see this line?" yelled a heavy set lady in a red shirt. "We have been out here for hours and we ain't inside yet! What's wrong up there? Somebody needs to fix this because we got little children out here. Y'all ain't gonna be happy until the winds come around here pickin' people up and throwing them on top the dome!" The woman was frustrated, as we all were. You could see the anger in her eyes right below the old emerald green head scarf she wore.

People waved and smiled at the cameras while others held their children up for the nation to see what was happening and to who it would really affect. The children were playing; they knew not of the danger they were truly facing. Tiny newborn babies, two possibly three weeks-old were innocently sleeping in their mothers' arms waiting.

There was a short single pregnant woman who looked young and as if she would pop at any moment who sat on the sidewalk behind us. She was alone and visibly afraid of what may happen to her and the child growing inside of her. New Orleans strangers soon became allies to her, assisting her up and down, and one even accompanying her to a secluded area for her to relieve herself during the long wait.

An older woman, seemingly in her seventies, sat in an aged wheelchair gripping the arm rest. Her hair was all white and her skin was filled with wrinkles. She was dazed and unaware of her surroundings. A black man, who didn't look much younger than my grandma, sat on the curb wearing a dingy navy blue backpack, held on to one of the wheels of the chair to prevent the old lady from moving.

The clouds began to grow dark and scary. The loud claps of thunder terrified us all. Children were told to halt and return to the arms of their guardians. It looked as if the rain was slowly making its way. I tried not to pay it too much mind but the sounds scared me. My grandmother nor my grandfather could protect me, I was alone in those moments. I tried to turn my back to the noise but it continued to tap me on the shoulder as if demanding I look in its direction. Small screams of terror filled the crowd, I had never seen New Orleans like this in the rain.

In my act of pretending the storm was not present a photographer passed by taking photos of a sad little girl attempting to reach the end of the line. Her hair went uncombed and her dirty Elmo shirt was covered in what one would assume was that day's breakfast. Her parents followed close behind seemingly enjoying the events. She carried an old gray teddy bear and tried to ignore the camera being pushed in her face. The little girl's eyes began to water but her mother did not stop what was happening, instead she encouraged it to continue. Maybe it was the lack of knowledge in the level of pain her daughter was facing or maybe they were just concentrating on getting to the back of the line.

While the mother did glance down at the photographer every now and again the father did not. He kept his head up high and continued to walk straight. Maybe it was his arrogance or maybe it was to keep the tears from leaving his eyes. Whatever it was, he wasn't planning on showing more than his stern expression to the world.

I watched as they reached the back where more family seemed to be waiting for their arrival. The photographer finally dashed off with his Nikon in order to freeze more memories. He began to follow another little girl with just her mother. The girl looked scared just as the first one did. However, this one was upset because she had just gotten a beating from her mother for running into the street.

We could feel the line inching towards the entrance. As the line moved, I could see National Guardsmen standing around. None of them seemed happy to be there nor appeared to be locals who enlisted, unless a uniform can change a person. They held their weapons close to their chest and some on their hips. I couldn't let go of the thoughts of why all of that was needed. Why did they want their weapons? We weren't getting ready for a war; we were hiding from a storm.

It was something about the way they looked at us. Like we were prisoners lining up to be thrown into a jail cell. Like we were animals on our last walk to the slaughter house. It made me feel like they weren't there to help us. They seemed so uncomfortable which made me feel the same instead of safe.

As the skies blacken even more and the clouds rolled quickly overhead, the crowd became disorderly and uncontrollable. Then with the bat of an eyelash and without any warning giant rain drops fell from the clouds. The smell of the rainstorm filled the air. So many "Oh no's" and "awe's" filled the area. Everyone pulled out something to cover their heads or ran to the sides to get out of the rain. The three of us didn't do either, we just stood there like soldiers. Wet, cold, hungry, frustrated soldiers. It may have been painful but we were not going to lose our spots. My granddad would not allow it. He wanted us to be inside and nothing was going to take his mind off of that. Not the rain pouring on top of us or the loud clapping of nature behind us. Nothing was going to get that man to move. He told my grandma not to move and she held my arm. I did make a desperate attempt to preserve the dryness of my cell phone. It was our only connection with the rest of the world. It was a life line I didn't want to lose.

The rain didn't stop. It slowed but it kept coming. The crowd couldn't take it anymore. They couldn't take the rain, they couldn't take the wind, and they couldn't take the cameras being pushed into our personal space, the little that we had left. They decided to take the long wait into their own hands.

"Let us in!"

"Let us in!"

The shouts grew louder and louder as they went on,

"Let us in!"

"Let us in!"

They pushed a little. Then they pushed a little more. A few jumped out of line and began to shout words that were not appropriate for a certain age group in the crowd. The young faces in uniform were growing scared. You could almost see their hearts beating faster and faster underneath their protective gear.

The thoughts of rioting came through the minds of all three of us as we watched the events unfold. I didn't want somebody to push me to the ground giving half of Orleans Parish a chance to stump their footprints into my head. No one wanted to re-live the Rodney King riots of 1992 in downtown New Orleans that day, but I felt like it was going to happen at any moment.

The National Guard members finally got the group calm. They yelled out to everyone that they were going to try harder to get everyone inside with the rainstorm beginning to press harder at our doorbell. Their words eased me a little. Other members of the line spoke softer but was still enraged that the little personal belongings they had was still being soaked.

Reaching the front of the line, with less than one hundred people in front of us, we could easily see why it took hours to get all of the citizens inside. The guards were checking every bag, box, and stroller that walked in the door. They were looking for drugs, guns, and other items that should have been left at home. The guardsmen were attempting to keep the place safe and the population protected. Their safety concerns were for a good reason but their strategies had failed.

Out of nowhere, the line started to move swiftly. The guards had gotten word from someone to stop the full searches and let everyone pass. They opened the double doors and let us just walk right in. No more checking bags and no more asking questions. Without the search in affect I'm sure some people had got in with their knives and drugs to keep them either safe or high. Some would be protected in their own mind while others were left naked and afraid.

When we got inside the freezing air attacked our bodies giving me the feeling of thousands of tiny needles sticking me all over. Chills ran up and down our frames before the National Guardsmen lined the hallway and directed us to the football field. The Superdome looked so clean and smelled fresh as if it was untouched. It was my first time in the Superdome and I was amazed at what I had seen so far. The structure, which had just turned 40 only a few weeks before, stunned me.

The last guardsmen pointed us to the New Orleans Saints football field. The ground felt different under my feet. The turf was nothing I had felt before. I took a moment to bend down to touch it with my hand to see what it felt like. The grass was fake, but the experience was very real. I couldn't wait to get back to school to tell everyone I touched the same field the city's football team did. I stood up and kept walking in the path I was directed. My grandparents were so astonished themselves they didn't even notice I had stopped.

There I walked on the fifty-yard line. The exact spot where the New Orleans Saints played their opponents. Where many games were won and lost; tears of both joy and sorrow were shed. The place Drew Brees would soon enough call home and make this city whole again. But in that moment, when I looked up into the stands, I told myself these were not memories I would want to remember. I could feel it in my bones this was not a time I would want to store on my internal hard drive.

I looked up and thousands of faces looked right back at me. Lights shined down on the field. The seats were filling with people in need and with nothing left to lose. I felt the world go quiet. People stopped moving, there was no more sound. It was me, my suitcase, and the fake grass beneath my feet. I felt alone again. My grandpa pulled me back to reality and told me to open up the luggage that I had managed to drag through all of the ciaos. We laid our thrift store bought blanket down on the phony turf and sat down. I sat next to my grandmother who had already pulled out her Bible. We then started our wait for what was promised to us; the storm of the century. The storm that would reshape the history of New Orleans forever. Katrina.

# Chapter 4: A Mother's Tattoo

*'To describe my mother would be to write about a hurricane in its perfect power. Or the climbing, falling colors of a rainbow"*

**-Maya Angelou**

I pulled the car over to the side of the bridge on my son's third birthday. My eyes created a lake of tears and I could no longer see the lines on the road clearly due to the words that had just left my middle sister's, Kendra, lips. It was shocking to hear what Kendra had told me but honestly it wasn't something I wouldn't expect "that woman" who is our biological mother to say.

We had just finished eating his birthday breakfast at Waffle House in Jacksonville, FL and were on our way back to Virginia. All morning I was getting text messages from my two younger sisters, Bre and Jayda, about how our mother thought I was the cause of all the sorrow. I was the reason we could no longer be a family and that I was keeping her grandson and their nephew away from them. I was never trying to keep him away from my sisters though, it was more so from our mother Yolanda, but I had my reasons. The woman was pure evil!

I had cried so many times before that day I can't even remember them all. I tried to avoid it. I tried to not hurt but I just couldn't fight the pain. I remember crying because she didn't show for my 25th birthday dinner. Looking at that empty chair made me understand she

49

would never be there for me. Yet again, I was alone, drowning in my own tears with my son staring at me from his car seat in the back. Kendra had just told me the wickedness our mother really had in her heart which helped me somewhat grasp that I was doing the right thing by keeping my son away. While her story for giving me up had something to do with a window and a pot, the reason she abandoned my middle sisters was something much more sinister.

Kendra suffered from epilepsy in which nerve cell activity in a person's brain is disturbed ultimately causing seizures. Yolanda being the mother that she is had left Kendra and Monyia, another sister of ours, to avoid the responsibility of a "sick kid." Kendra overheard the conversation between Yolanda and her father many years before. My heart couldn't take anymore. I had suffered for so many years alone, afraid and wanting so badly to be apart of a family, a sister to sister friendship, anything at all to fill that emptiness and she was just giving family away. I wasn't offered that chance and nor were my baby sisters. We were without each other and without our mother.

I was thirteen when I sat in the bathroom on the toilet with lip gloss in one hand, eye shadow in the other, and some tampons a school mate had given me in my bag on the floor. Just thinking about if my grandpa knew I had those tampons instead of pads, I would have gotten a talking to about sticking things in my lady area that God wouldn't approve of. He thought using tampons and any other feminine hygiene product was more of a sexual thing than feminine health. I never thought to explain to him what it was really for or to challenge his authority.

I got up from my shinny white seat and walked over to the mirror. I tried to put the makeup on myself like the other girls. My lips were too shiny and the eye shadow made me look like the clown from Steven King's famous movie "IT" rather than a mature young lady. I gazed at myself and the caked on greasepaint covering my skin and started to cry. I didn't know what I was doing. I was lost in this process and I just didn't know what to do.

Quickly, I wiped my tears because there were more important tasks at hand. Lifting the seat cover of the toilet, I thought of what I was about to do next. I pulled down my pants and underwear and had a seat. I opened the bag and saw four tampons. I picked the first one up, took off the wrapping, pushed the cotton out of the applicator and tried to insert it into myself. That didn't work at all, I guess the blue plastic part was named applicator for a reason. I opened the second one and tried again but it hurt me so bad I had to stop. Two more times I tried to complete the task but both were unsuccessful. I put my head in the palm of my hands and started crying once again. I was furious, disappointed, and depressed. I just wanted to be normal and fit in with all the other girls at school.

Earlier that day someone made it very clear that I was not normal. I started to wish I could be like this one girl in my school who had fair skin and a tiny build. She was the prettiest seventh grader I had ever seen. She couldn't be more than 5'5" while I was already five foot eight inches and considered the beast of our class. She had the nicest smile and I envied her. Her parents had allowed her to dye her hair to a deep burgundy. It was long, shiny, and looked so soft brushing against her face.

That day she asked me if I knew how to use makeup. Those were pretty much the only words she had ever spoken to me the whole year. I thought she was trying to be friendly or even show me how but I found out it was all a plan to belittle me. She began to spread the word that I didn't know how to use the basic necessities a normal girl had learned to use years before their teens. She told all our classmates I had no friends and I had never even used a tampon. I thought I could share these things with her because of her sweet smile but I was wrong.

I hate to admit it, but it was true. It was evil how she said it but there were no lies. I wasn't even allowed to have make up. The friends I thought I did have were not, at least not at that school. The pretty popular girl knew before I even told her I had never used tampons before. She and her friends put it together a long time ago. My uniform pants that were bought from a nearby thrift store were so tight that the group of girls could see the outlining of a pad. They pointed and laughed at me saying I was a baby wearing a diaper.

Another girl in my class stepped in to defend me by handing me some makeup to practice with and a handful of women hygiene products. I know she wanted to be friends with the popular girls but just didn't have the heart to see the torture they were subjecting me to.

"Tyierra," the girl started as she held my hand, "don't let them do that shit to you. Take this and try it yourself. They just mad because you don't need no makeup."

52

Her efforts had gone to waste. I was crying in the bathroom on the toilet with makeup smeared all over my face and half used tampons thrown all over the floor. I was a fool to think I could do this on my own. I needed my mother.

When I was born, my mother, for the lack of a better option, gave me away to her mother and stepfather who became my illegal guardians, yes illegal. Yolanda told me at one point it was because she didn't have anything to give me. Her exact words were, "Tyierra, I didn't have a pot to piss in or a window to throw it out of. I couldn't take you. I needed to get me right." That was a phrase I would carry with me my entire life; words I would grow to hate.

For a long time, I had nothing in my heart but hate for Yolanda. Every day for eighteen years, I saw something that reminded me of the fact that I was without the one thing every little girl needed. If it wasn't the lack of advice about how to handle myself around bullies, like the girls who teased me about makeup and tampons, it was not informing me what was right and wrong when it came to relationships.

All of the training I was supposed to be given by the mother figure in a child's life was taught to me by the TV set, the internet, or by accident. In the sixth grade I learned what a proper lady looked like. My sixth grade teacher, Mrs. Gwindalyn Bellizan, is who I studied while she walked in her fancy heels and how she spoke intellectually with those around her. She was also the person to give me a pad when I got my cycle for the first time in the middle of her class. Television mom Clair Huxtable was also more of a mother to me than anyone else. She was the one who taught me that I shouldn't let what a man brings to the table be all that I eat. I also learned that you shouldn't be afraid to be direct and when all else fails make sure you look good.

While I love my grandmother dearly, she was not the person I referred to for things like my period, relationships, or how to be self-reliant. Grandma Ludie didn't want me to take a shower or bath during my five-day cycle each month. She thought the shock of water "entering my system" would kill me. Instead, she handed me a face towel and told me to wipe off. Every boy was the devil to her or was going to take me away. It was a living inferno. Instead of asking for her help on an issue, I would just wait on the newest episode of The Proud Family on Disney.

Neither of my grandparents were connected to the time period I was. There was no one who could teach me the basics. It may be hard to believe but I didn't even learn to tie my shoes until I was nine. I was stuck out in this world almost on my own. All I really wanted was a mother to take me under her wings. Instead, I was a kid who was locked away for most of her childhood guessing at what to do next. But no matter what, I always had hope.

I didn't know where she was most of the time. Yolanda would call my grandma about once every two years. I had only come face to face with Yolanda about four times before I turned eighteen. All I knew about her was that she was a solider in the US Army and I had four sisters, in which I had met only two of them. Monyia I had seen as a baby and Bre who I met when I was almost ten. Monyia and Kendra, grew up in the Los Angeles area with their father while Bre and Jayda were with Yolanda. I was so desperate to see all of them and be a family. At fifteen I got my mother's email address from my aunt. I figured this was going to be my chance to reach out and get her to want to be in my life. I was going to write her and spill my heart out and she would finally want that dream of a happy family too. I wrote a long email explaining to her how I felt. I got a response with very few words but two of them were "call me."

A week before Katrina was to make landfall and change the lives of countless people forever, I found myself on the phone with my mother. She had been stationed in Georgia, a short drive to New Orleans and I could fill the sprinkle of a connection between a mother and child growing. The early conversation gave me the same feeling you get when you talk on the phone with your crush for the first time. I was nervous and excited all at once. I just knew she would want to be my mother now. Her voice was soft and sweet as if her words floated from her lips. She was well spoken and very proper, unlike those in New Orleans. I couldn't believe I was speaking with my mother!

After a few weeks of random phone calls the summer of 2005, she finally told me she would venture to NOLA to rescue me from my grandparents. We had gone so far into the dream of me being her daughter that we had started to make plans for my 16th birthday that was a few short months away; getting my nails done for the first time and even teaching me how to drive. I would finally get to be with my mother. I was going to get a chance to be normal.

I decided I would need to pack a small bag to take with me. I didn't have many possessions but there were a few things I didn't want to go without. Neither of my grandparents knew what was going on. I didn't even tell them I was talking to her much but instead said it was just some classmates from school. I didn't want to upset my grandmother, as she would not have been able to take the news of me leaving. I planned for it to be a lot smoother to just go and not drag it out.

Yolanda's words I still hear in my sleep, "I'm coming to get my baby! I will be there tomorrow morning. Mommy is coming to get you."

The night before her supposed arrival, I remember being filled with eagerness and panic. The feeling was the same as those you feel when you are on that long climb at the beginning of a roller coaster ride; it is a chilling sensation, but you know you will be happy you experienced it at the end of the ride.

I thought to myself in less than 24 hours I am going to be with my mom and my sisters. Finally! We are going to be a normal family. I am going to be a normal girl. I packed a couple things every top of the hour so not to alert my snooping grandmother. First, it was a book I got during the school year I liked; "Of Mice and Men." Then, I put a couple pair of socks and some earrings I got in my bag that I didn't have the matching backs to. I just used the erasers to my pencils to keep them on. Before dark came over New Orleans I was packed and ready to go. I called my mother one last time. She answered.

"Hello?"

"Hey! How are you?" I asked.

"Good, good. You packed and ready to go tomorrow? Did you tell them yet?" I could tell she was driving while talking to me. Her turning signal was singing loudly in the background.

I ran to the small closet where my bag was being stored. I jumped in and closed the door behind me. I tried to grip the phone tighter and push it closer to my face. I didn't want anyone to know my plans just yet. "Yes, I packed but I didn't tell them. I'm just gonna wait until you get here to let them know. What time will you be here?" My heart was knocking on my chest.

"Well," there was a long pause before she replied. It was if she hadn't come up with a set plan just yet, "I should be there around noon. It's going to be a Sunday so there should be no traffic."

We talked about ten minutes more about what fun things there are to do in Georgia before saying our goodbyes. I went to bed early that Saturday night so to be well rested for the drive back with her. I didn't want her to fall asleep driving because no one was keeping her awake. My grandparents did question my motives for going to bed so early on a Saturday. Usually, I would be up late watching murder mysteries or writing poems and short stories. My reasoning, of course I decided I didn't want to share. I wouldn't dare break their hearts, not right now.

I woke early the next day with a smile on my face. The anticipation didn't want me to sleep any longer. Looking at the time it was only 6:38 in the morning. I wrote in my tiny journal all the excitement that was scheduled to occur in hours to come. Thank goodness my grandparents hadn't found a church to go to in the area just yet or I would have been up already. I got on my feet, ran through my morning routine and waited. I glanced through the blinds every now and again to see if she had arrived early. I called a few times to see if she needed my voice as company but got no answer. I figured she just didn't want to be distracted on the road.

Noon came around and there was no sign of Yolanda. I wasn't worried when I didn't see her car in front of our apartment. Most people aren't on time when traveling. Stopping for food, restroom breaks, and the occasional city traffic could mess up anyone's travel plans. I told myself to give her a two-hour window. I just sat on the floor facing the closet where my packed bag was and ate my chips and cookies. I knew she would be there at any moment. I just had to wait. She was coming.

It's been fifteen years I can bare a few more hours.

It wasn't until eight hours later and sixteen calls to Yolanda's phone that I realized that I had been tricked, deceived, and cheated. Just like the thousands of times before, she was not where she said she would be. She wasn't with me. She wasn't coming! I didn't cry this time. I pushed my bag to the back of my closet, placed the phone on the charger, and tucked myself under the blankets. My grandmother was sitting on the edge of the bed we shared reading her Bible when I got in. She looked at me and smiled. She got up from her seat, walked over to me and placed a kiss on my head.

"You okay, baby?" she asked as she patted me on my arm that was covered by my blanket.

I fluffed my pillow some trying to distract my eyes from shedding any pointless tears. "I'm fine. Thank you."

She tilted her head to the side, "Thank me for what?"

"For asking me if I'm okay," I replied softly.

"Oh, that's what mammas do baby. Get some rest. Mamma loves you."

"I love you, too," I closed my eyes to sleep.

My cellphone started to ring close to midnight. It wasn't loud. Thank goodness for that. I didn't want anyone to think some boy was calling me. The caller was Yolanda. Seeing her name rejuvenated me and I sprung out of the bed. I pressed the talk button.

"Hello? You here?" I said faintly. I hiked over to the blinds and searched for a car that she might have drove. My grandmother was fast asleep in the bed I was just in but did not feel me remove myself.

Silence over took the conversation before she spoke, "I'm not coming. I caught a flat about half way there and I didn't want to drive the rest of the way on a spare tire so I just turned around to get a new tire and I'm not gonna be able to come get you right now. With my job and then your sister going through this whole thing with her dad and…"

It's okay," I interrupted, "I already figured you weren't going to come. I gotta get up for school tomorrow. I will talk to you about it some other time." I hung up the call without even saying good-bye and got back in the bed. I was angry but too tired and already half sleep. I couldn't put any more energy into that woman. Not that night. I just couldn't handle it anymore.

I didn't hear anything from her again until 2008 about two weeks before I graduated high school when she got wind that I was joining the military. Maybe she thought I wanted to follow in her footsteps or maybe she was proud her oldest had completed something. I didn't care either way. The hell she had let me face with Katrina when only seven days before it could have been prevented if she came and got me like she said she would, there was nothing that would get me to ever like that woman.

She bought me an engraved congratulations paperweight and sent it to me in the mail. I decided to keep it because it was the only thing she had ever given me besides my name. I packed a box of stuff that I would have my grandma send to me after boot camp. I placed the small token right on top of all the photos, poems, and other memories I had. Right on top, was the paperweight, the one thing I thought I could not live without.

By the time I finished boot camp and had been assigned a duty station in Virginia Beach, VA, Yolanda had gotten station at Fort Lee, only a couple hours away. Now I had a car to drive to her. I was going to make her my mom for real this time. The hate seemed to have vanished with the thought of a possible better future dancing around in my head.

Only a few months as a resident of VA, I found myself standing in the mud room of my mother in Hopewell, VA. Visiting Yolanda felt like visiting an older sister rather than a mom. She greeted me at the door, still in her uniform from work. She gave me a big hug and then grabbed my backside.

"Dang, woman!" She yelled out, "Where did you get all that hip from?"

I smiled and didn't comment on it. That was a weird hello I thought to myself. I took a look around her lovely home planted in a newly build neighborhood. It was a sight to see. With four bedrooms, fully carpeted, and high ceilings it was the most beautiful house I had ever been in. I was use to studio apartments with roaches, hardly any running water, and no power. Her house was like visiting 1600 Pennsylvania Avenue to me.

I was proud to see someone in this family could go out and buy a house, buy and own anything really! Someone was stable enough to raise a family in one place. Someone who didn't have to worry about someone else coming to kick them out on the first of the month because the rent wasn't paid. That thought made me so happy. Then the same thought made me a bit outraged. That was the life I was supposed to be living! Instead, my childhood was the complete opposite.

Yolanda excused herself for a few moments to change out of her military gear. I watched as she walked away in her uniform and towards the stairs. She stood about 5'7'' with an athletic build. She was much darker than I was, her chocolate colored coating was smooth and tight. She hid her hair under a short cut wig to remain in uniform regulation. She looked nothing like the forty something year olds I've ever seen. She was a beautiful, happy woman and always tried to keep her body in shape. She would do a five-mile run every morning and made it known she would never be the fat kid. Unlike my sisters, I look very little like my mother. The only features we really share are our eyes and our smiles. Those high cheek bones were hereditary.

When she returned I saw more of my mother's silky skin in a comfortable tank top and jeans. Yolanda had a few noticeable tattoos. I had only gotten one at the time and wasn't sure if I wanted others because of how painful it was. In polite conversation with her over our first dinner together, I mentioned my concerns to her about getting inked.

"Don't be a baby now! You can take a little pain. Look at the tattoos I have," she pointed out the different tattoos all over her body and their meaning. Most of them were normal and nothing fancy. Although the one she eventually got on her wrist really did say, "Fancy." Then I saw it. She turned around to have her back facing me and I saw the tattoo. This one tattoo in particular, unlike the others really caught my eye.

When I saw it on her back, year 2009, I knew then that she would never be my real mother. At the nape of her neck was a cute little tattoo that will be etched in my heart forever. She had the names of only two of the five daughters she had. Of course it was of the two girls that lived with her. It was still a lot to take in. Five kids and only two names? I couldn't believe she would do that. Did she forget that she has three other children before the two painted on her back? Or did she erase us from her memory?

My throat was dry, my eyes started to water, and my heart skipped a few beats. I could feel my eyes starting to bleed. I excused myself to the restroom to gather myself. I entered the half bath in my mother's beautiful home and stared at myself in the mirror. There I was again, in a mirror drowning in my own tears.

For a long time, I continued to try and build something with her. After receiving numerous awards, inviting her to the events, and her constantly not showing I still tried. After she accused me of having a baby just to get her attention I still tried. I wanted for so long to be a part of my mother that it started to hurt me deeply. I thought I needed her in order for me to be the best version of myself but I think a little part of me died that day. The little girl who use to want so desperately for that connection left when I saw my mother's tattoo.

# Chapter 5: When Nothing Goes Right, Go Left

*"As long as poverty, injustice and gross inequality exist in our world, none of us can truly rest."*
**-Nelson Mandela**

The wet and cold people in the crowd including us were finally shown to a seat in the bleachers and off the field. We were confused to why we had to move but I just grabbed the thin blanket we had and marched in the direction they pointed. It was very calm at first glance but over crowded. People had started to arrive with large groups of family and friends. Most of them were dragging around luggage that took up most of the spaces. Others had pulled out bedspreads to protect themselves from the freezing cold AC blowing in the Superdome. A young black woman with a black and gold silk scarf draped around her head was finishing up the last two braids of her young daughter's hair. I'm sure she must have started before the mayor's announcement to evacuate the Crescent City.

Both of my grandparents could not find comfort in the seats made of hard plastic. Their bodies required something easier to sit on with a lot more cushion. Even with the seats and their unwelcome hardness, everyone was just happy to be out of Katrina's winds and rain.

We just sat and people watched, observing everyone around who ended up in the same situation as us. There were so many different, fresh faces surrounding me. So many individuals in the city I had never had the pleasure of meeting before. I sat and thought about what they all had going on outside of the dome walls. Did they have children? Did they go to college? How about their favorite movies? I even started to think about the bad in their lives. I wondered if they were struggling the same way that we were and if they had to keep secrets from family and friends as well.

I thought about a tall white man sitting four rows below us being a convicted felon. The thought scared me to think that I may be surrounded by people who murdered little light skinned girls in their sleep. I tried to redirect my mind to something else so that I didn't go into a panic and have my heart fall out of my chest.

I was sitting next to my grandmother who was flipping the pages of her old worn out Good Book. She had written phone numbers all over the edges of the thin sheets of paper that made up the sixty-six stories of the Bible. It was the only possession of hers that she would never forget if she had to make a quick getaway because of unpaid rent. My grandfather sat and starred off into the bleachers that were slowly being filled by New Orleans citizens. His face was filled with disappointment and frustration. I could almost read his mind. He felt left.

His son had abandoned him in his time of need. He couldn't protect my grandmother or me from what was coming next. All he could do was already being done; sit and wait. Wait until the storm passes. Wait until they say the great beast of a hurricane turned back into the gulf and avoided land altogether and we can return home. Just wait it out. So wait we did.

I decided to pull out my huge purple textbook I was lugging around. I had to finish the homework I was assigned the Friday morning before. I figured I should use this time wisely and complete my assignments instead of wondering about the past of those people around me. On Tuesday morning, I was going to be right back inside my classroom at McMain and that homework was still going to be due with no excuses seeing that we had an extra day to work on it.

I remember getting to the ninth question of my worksheet before someone dressed in military gear marched to the middle of the field with a microphone in his head. His uniform was well decorated and I can remember thinking to myself that he seemed a little old to be in the military. His hair was snow white and his skin covered in wrinkles. As he checked to see if the microphone was working properly, he smiled into the crowd of faces preparing to hear him speak. If he was nervous, it was not seen in his approach. His confidence convinced me whatever words that were about to spill out of his mouth would be nothing but the truth.

"How's everybody doing tonight?" he asked as if he were about to perform for us or tell us some long drawn out dirty jokes on a comedy tour, "I am glad to see so many faces. Amazing how we get a better turn out today than during the football season," he gave a short chuckle. Some were amused but a lot of the Saints fans there were not. "Well, anyway we are here to help you if you need us. Anything you want just ask one of us."

"We want to go home!" somebody howled from the crowd, making everybody laugh, I'm sure making the man front and center was a little jealous that his one-liner didn't get the same reaction.

"Well I don't think I can do anything about that but anything else we're happy to assist. We also want to let you know that we will be serving meals today for you guys. Nice little surprise right? Isn't that nice?" everyone cheered and clapped, "We will begin serving in a few minutes and we're going to go by section. I ask that everyone just be patient with us."

He began to talk about how the house keeping was expected to be handled and he touched on safety. It felt like the preflight safety demonstration that no one thinks they should pay attention to anymore because they've heard it a hundred times. A lot of us could hear him but not many were listening. He then explained that there was food for everyone, but we needed to proceed to the pickup locations by sections. After his remarks, he exited the field.

My granddaddy walked up the steep stairs to get some food even though our section was one of the last to be called. He wanted to get in there before the rush or before they run out of food. He saw that they really weren't listening to proper order anyway. It was every man for themselves.

Sitting there waiting on my grandpa's return, I began to people watch again, mostly to avoid that homework assignment that I thought would be simple and turned out not to be. Many of the people there had brought their whole lives with them. About two rows above us, there was a young white couple, noticeably New

Orleans natives, cuddled together under their blanket. They were looking at old photographs of happy memories that had come and gone. To the right of us, there were young kids talking between themselves and playing hand games. Their mother was on a search for food like my grandpa.

A few older African-American ladies to the left were holding hands with each other praying to God in hopes that He will spare the lives of every person in the city. I could see the want to join them in my grandma's big brown eyes but she fought the need to get up and begin a prayer circle with the aged women. This was a new experience for me but it wasn't fear I was feeling. To be honest, I'm not sure what it was. Empty or hollow are the only words that could describe the mood my spirit was carrying. I felt as if I had no purpose anymore.

When my granddaddy came back from the line, nearly forty-five minutes later, he had a brown rectangle shaped thing in his hand. It looked like a tan popcorn bag. It was definitely something I had never seen before.

"What's that?" I asked with a look of disgust on my face.

"It's food," he handed it to me and I gazed at it as if it were going to start talking to me.

"It's a MRE, meal ready to eat. It's military food. It's decent and it's free." My grandpa had been a solider in the Army for a little less than four years long before I was born. I was barely seven when I saw my grandma use scotch tape to poster my grandpa's photo to the apartment wall. He was a very attractive military man in his younger days. That photo was long gone by now. The apartments we lived in where it was hanging on display had evicted us and changed the locks while we were out. We weren't able to get any of our belongings and all the photo memories we had would have been thrown out.

After being kicked out of our apartment in East New Orleans, my grandpa found us shelter in a house that stood right behind his job. He told us that his boss also owned the small unattractive two bedroom building but I never took it as truth. I think he lied to my grandmother to make her feel safe in a not so safe place. It was an old unleveled shot gun house. The once white paint was chipping on every side and there was no yard, the grass knew nothing of the dirt around it. It reminded me of photos of old abandon buildings in the middle of nowhere that you would see frozen in black and white. No color was present. Just old plastered unwanted building material holding together by school glue and prayers. But for us three, it was something since we had nothing else.

I'm not even sure if his employer even knew that we were living there as we had to pack up everything every morning before we left. My granddad would go right next door and begin his day of work while my grandmother and I would just ride the bus around during the day since I wasn't enrolled in school. There were days she would bring me to work with her at a Winn-Dixie that was nearby. I remember she would tuck me away in the middle of a floor display made out of cases of strawberry and peach Chek soda, a New Orleans favorite.

I would pretend that I was a princess in a castle waiting on all my little princess friends to come over. I would make-believe I was throwing a huge formal ball that everybody in the land was invited to, even my servants. There would be tea and little lemon squares. Once my imaginary gown was on and my fictitious decorations were up, I would sit there and wait for my guest. I would just wait and wait, and then I would snap back and realized no one was ever coming.

When I wasn't riding around on the RTA city bus or fighting off made-up dragons in my thirst-quenching palace, I was in that tiny house right off Washington and Broad. It was a nothing shack but we called it home for a little while. I can remember watching the candlelight dancing on the soiled walls because there was no power.

I can still hear the sounds from my mother pulling weeds out of the ground that had wiggled through the loose flooring. One of the rooms had no floor at all. It was just bare concrete. We avoided that room but it made little difference. The house was still something that should have been knocked down a long time ago. The tub was designed with dirt rings circling it and the sink constantly dripped. My grandma and grandpa slept with their backs to the wall facing the front door to ensure no one would come barging in at night.

The locks were not very reliable there and the door didn't really close as it was intended to. I would sleep in one of their laps wrapped in a red and white blanket my uncle had given me to feel safe. There was no bed for me to lie on. There was absolutely nothing at all. Grandpa Burnell had shared that the living arrangements were only temporary and there was no need to get furniture brought there.

There was a draft coming from under all the doors and a few of the windows in the rear were shattered. This was the worst place I had ever lived. I felt like a homeless person. At six I could still remember I was feeling like no one cared for me and I wasn't even allowed to ask for help. My grandma told me not to share with anyone where I lived and I didn't for two reasons. One, I was afraid that what my grandparents had told me, that some people would take me from them and place me in some old white woman's house as a foster child, would actually happen. Being taken away from them was one of the biggest fears they shackled me with. Secondly, I had no one to tell.

I would just sit on my blanket very quietly and eat my food that I was given. Most of the time it was a ham sandwich, more like a slice of ham and two slices of bread and other times I would get watery tuna. I ate so much ham and bacon as a kid that I refuse to eat it now. There were, however, a few moments in my childhood I was faced with sugar sandwiches, where my mother would put a spoon full of sugar between two slices of bread. The same went for syrup and ketchup sandwiches. But it made me happy. I got to eat all this sweet stuff and no one told me to stop. That sugar sandwich was my little piece of heaven even though I still could feel the hunger in my belly after I was done. If you go to that spot now, where that old house stood, you would find yourself in an old empty lot. The building has been knocked down since Katrina, rightfully so.

But there we sat, in the bleachers, holding those MREs. I thought back to sitting on that concrete floor eating that offensive ham sandwich. Nothing could be worst than that. But I still didn't eat anything out of my MRE. I figured it would be there tomorrow or I could just wait until Tuesday when we were free to leave the Superdome to eat. I've waited longer than that before.

Instead, I just went to sleep to rest myself. I had realized that I was about to face my monthly woman issues with painful cramps twisting away at my stomach. My granddad watched as I tucked my wrapped meal into the extra space in my bag right next to my textbook. My bag was growing full of things I really didn't want.

I leaned on my grandmother's shoulder. I decided to take a nap to fight my hunger and take my mind off the waiting. I hoped to be waken up by a tap from my grandparents telling me it was time to go home. I was ready to go back to our small apartment and put on my uniform of black and gold and be on my way to school. I would just do that last little bit of my homework on the bus that day on the way to class. After my grandmother wiggled a little to make herself comfortable, I drifted off to dreamland.

I was dragged out of my deep sleep by a small soft touch on my cheek. Then another and another. Liquid kisses stared to touch my face over and over.

Is my grandfather playing jokes on me? Because I'm really not in the mood right now!

My grandfather was good at messing with me in my sleep. In the sixth grade he convinced me that I had wet the bed. My sheets were soaked due to him pouring a cup of warm water in the bed just for a good chuckle. I went an entire day thinking I had wet myself somehow before he eventually told me while waiting at the bus stop.

I soon realized that silky tapping on me was not my grandfather but rather the rain that Katrina had dragged in with her. The white covering on the top of the dome had started to rip off and the rain was pouring in on us. You could hear parts of the dome whipping in the wind and the pieces that were barely staying attached banging on the roof. It was small room temperature splashes all over my body. With the mix of cold air in the dome, we were beginning to freeze. The rain pouring in was the first sign of us not being able to return to our homes on the next day but it was not the last.

Sitting up in my seat, I watched as people rushed upward to protect themselves from the storms tears. I saw flaps of the Superdome's skin beating the top of the building. The wind whistled loudly as it ran in and out of the well-known fully exposed arena. When the lights flickered off, I heard people scream from afar that the dome would not make it through the storm. They were afraid the roof would be torn off and gusts of wind would suck us right from inside to face the hell of Katrina. The lights were soon restored but that's when we all knew that we were living on the power from a backup generator. No longer would the refrigerators that held the food supply work. The air conditioning wouldn't continue to blow out the freezing air and the visibility in places where natural light never touched, like the bathrooms, would be destroyed.

My mother grabbed our suitcase and then my hand to hurry me. We stood there for a while as downpour made the seats below seem like little lakes. The field was now drenched in rain. I could still see some people struggling to protect themselves but only prolonging their need to move to dry ground.

As we watched the down poor and heard the roof peel away, members of the National Guard began to arrive. They soon guided us to a tunnel that I didn't know the dome even had but then again, this was my first visit inside of any football arena so everything around me was new and unknown. It was more of a ramp I assumed used for easy travel from one level to another or could have been for larger deliveries.

"Right this way! Right this way!" one man in uniform kept yelling into the crowd pointing for us all to go left. Going right would cause some pedestrian traffic delays. The guardsman reminded me of someone from TV escorting a group of rich and swanky people to their seats to watch an opera or eat a lavish steak and lobster dinner. There was nothing lavish about where we had ended up though.

The three of us found a good spot on the floor in a corner. Soon the area around us began to fill up. To our right was a family of six. To our left, there was a couple who had just had a newborn baby. They didn't speak very much English. Across from us was a young man, a younger lady, and their three children, two of them old enough to walk.

A little ways down the hall was a middle aged woman alone with her newborn. She was surrounded by three bags of diapers and formula. She didn't look as young as the other mothers in the hallway but not old enough to be a grandmother either. All of us were wet and frustrated, including the children. The moment was damp, emotionless, and terrifying but we had to face it. We had to dry off and prepare for what was ahead. What was worst, my homework and school book was now drenched. I never did get a chance to finish that assignment.

# Chapter 6: Nothing Changes if Nothing Changes

*If history repeats itself, and the unexpected always happens, how incapable must man be of learning from experience."*
**-George Bernard Shaw**

Sitting on the floor of the dome made me think of all the different places I've lived in while being in New Orleans. House after house. Apartment after apartment. There were three different houses we lived in on Louisiana Avenue Parkway in Uptown. I can remember at least eight right off the top of my head without even thinking in the third ward alone. With my grandfather having such a horrible gambling problem, there was a constant struggle to keep a roof over our head. It was if history had repeated itself right there in the Superdome. I remember thinking it was going to be just another struggle for me to fight through.

The dark, sticky, and cold ramp reminded me of so many of the places I had already lived. To some that moment in the dome, realizing that there may be nothing outside those walls soon and the little they did have could be floating in the middle of the street somewhere was a scary feeling. I, on the other hand, was use to this touch of fear and felt quite comfortable and warm. Being homeless or damn near close to it, having no water or power, and being without food were things that were considered normal in my world.

This was the life that the God, who my grandma praised so much, had given to me. I was taught that it was okay to live life this way. This was... my normal. I was confused in my younger years as I was anything but normal. While all the other children around me were full, clothed, and happy with those they lived with. My grandmother promised me my life was just as everyone else and it was going to be okay because God had a plan for us all. I just had to keep waiting.

To bring income in to pay for housing my grandmother had her own ways of making quick cash. She would buy lotto tickets every few weeks or so as she was more of a scratch off and slots kinda lady. Those lotto tickets were her most prized possessions. Her gambling was nothing compared to her life partner's obsession with the ponies though. She would buy ten, twenty, sometimes thirty tickets at once and put them in random places in her old worn down burgundy Bible. Her bible had a strap on it that was barely holding together anymore. The clasp to keep the Bible shut was nearly defeated as it had to keep the pages together, lotto tickets tucked safely, and photos of all of her family from falling out.

She would hand over her last few dollar bills to a lady behind a glass wall at the corner store and then look at me and say, "Baby, God will work it out. These numbers are gonna hit and I'm going to buy us a big house and I'ma get me a nice fancy car. God gone do his work for us." but those numbers never hit and God never did his work in the sense that my grandmother was looking for.

She insisted that if we gave our last to the church or the lotto quick picks, the last of the little that we had, and if we had faith and hope we will be alright.

We really lived life off of air, hopes, and faith. Living with them, I never really experienced being full however. I started to get jealous of the horses at the track and the ticket machine they chose to spend our last on, they were surely eating better than I was. I just wished someone would have noticed and was brave for me, but no one ever did. Even at school, where I got most of my meals, no one saw the problem. What they saw was not what I needed them to.

I remember I was starving one day while standing in the lunch line at school. It was around the last few days in April and my grandpa's funds from his Social Security check for the month had dried up. I didn't really talk to any of the people in my class. Starting school only a month before, for the first time, and I was seven didn't sit right with the other children. I was the weird dirty sandy redhead black girl who just showed up in the first grade. It was a strange situation.

A group of first graders stood in the lunch line in front and behind me. Huge fans sat on the floor blasted in my face as the Louisiana heat had already started to creep in with full force. I was inching closer and closer to the lunch trays and soon to the sitting area; a sitting area where only, a week before, while I ate the school provided breakfast, two rowdy male third graders threw syrup packets and plastic sporks at me from a neighboring table. I wasn't very attractive and it gave the kids around me an opportunity to not be nice. I was use to the behavior so I didn't report it to any of the teachers. It would only make the situation worst anyway. Not only would I be an ugly duckling but then I would be a tattletale also. It was just easier to forget what happened and deal with the abuse.

I hated being treated differently because I was older and strange. I hated that cafeteria. I hated school. I hated being there with people I knew didn't want me to be there but it was my only option. One thing I did love and looked forward to was the lunch. As nasty and unappealing as it was, I loved every bit of it. My grandma and grandpa sometimes struggled to feed our family. I remember lots of days when undercooked white rice was our main entrée, if we were blessed enough to get to it before the cockroaches did. If I was lucky, my grandma would even put sugar and butter on the rice for taste. Sometimes I would see dead bugs trapped in the sugar probably in efforts to discover their own meal as well. If it wasn't rice, I could always expect the sandwiches made of bread and syrup or a thin layer of sugar but it was never enough.

The school served breakfast and lunch wasn't that good but it did hold me over for a little while longer than bread dipped in sweet pancake liquid. Hints why I was excited to get the large scoop of unappetizing spaghetti slammed on my tan plastic tray, right next to soggy broccoli, and the individual carton of 2% milk. I walked slowly to ensure I didn't drop anything on the way towards my stool. A girl in my class was right behind me but decided to skip one of the seats and not sit next to me. She didn't even look at me when she did it. Maybe, just like the rest of the kids in the school, she did not want anyone to associate the two of us together.

I had no time for her or to attempt to find my feelings on how I truly felt about her unnecessary act. I turned to look down at my plate. I felt the rumble of my tiny tummy through my white school shirt. I also had peaches and a cookie along with all the other goodies that were sectioned off on my dish. I was in such a rush that I dropped my napkin in the juices that my peaches had made into their own pool. I had everything I needed in front of me, then I realized I forgot the most important part of eating a meal. I forgot my fork.

There was no time to go back now! I was starving. I would have to raise my hand to ask permission to go back and get the stupid utensil and that walk was through a terrible traffic jam of first, second, and third graders who would at some point push me or knock the fork out of my hand. Not to mention we only have a certain amount of allowed time to eat. What if I didn't have time to finish? So I did what any other person would do, or what a first grader would assume others would do. I used my hands.

I will admit now, thinking back, that it wasn't one of my brightest moments. At the time, in my mind, I thought it was the most logical way of getting that food from the plate to my mouth without causing any disturbance. The broccoli was the first to go. Although it was mushy and tasteless it worked for me and got the job done. I tried the cookie but it was a bit too hard for my liking so I put it aside. I was hungry but I still wanted to keep my teeth. I thought that once I opened my milk it would help me get it down but first, I wanted to get the rest of my meal out of the way.

Then came the spaghetti. It was sitting there like a scoop of ice cream because of the ice cream scoopers they used to serve our meals. I looked at it for a second to see how I would properly tame the saucy beast. I just picked it up in my hand like a warm baseball and started to bit into it. In between bites, I would use my other hand to throw a peach or two in my mouth. The taste of spaghetti sauce and peaches wasn't the best but the purpose was met each time. I was just hungry and nothing else mattered.

I could feel the eyes of the students around me, yet I did not attempt to stop. My body was in auto drive and it was like I couldn't control it. I was too hungry to stop. I didn't know if I was going to eat that night. I had to get in as much as I could as quickly as I could.

Everything was fine, or my version of fine, until one of the teachers spotted me from afar. Ms. Powers, one of the most respected third grade teachers at Andrew H. Wilson Elementary, and boy was she scary. At least she was scary to me as a first grader lost in what was real and what was not. She had white hair but her face looked so young. She was a cruel woman to people who didn't know her but I got to know her pretty well once I was placed in her class a few years later.

Ms. Powers walked up next to me. In this seemingly quiet room that was known to echo and said with all the might in her body, "Are you seriously eating with your hands!? That is disgusting!"

Everyone in there turned to look at me. First, second, and third graders just scrunched up their faces and made throw up motions. The sounds of "eww" filled the room. I lowered my head slowly and slammed the remaining of my meal on the plate. I attempted to ask if I could go and wash my hands and try to rectify the issue but was not allowed to do so. I did not finish my meal that day. I was too overwhelmed with shame.

I was curious to know if I was the only one in the room who was as hungry as I was at that moment. So hungry that taking three minutes to get a fork was pain. Was there just one more kid in that room feeling how I felt? Was there one more kid on my block who had to deal with the pain I had to deal with? The teasing, the hunger? Just one?

Food was only one of the things we too often found ourselves over and over going without. Water and lights were the most popular items on the list but somewhere to stay was not too far behind. We kept doing things the same way and expecting something completely different to happen, and it never did. Insanity is what some would call it. I called it my grandpa.

My family and I moved so much when I was young I never really got the chance to get comfortable in one place. When I was a little over eleven, I started living out of my backpack and refused to leave anything of importance in whatever house we were occupying. I was afraid that when I got out of school, the home I got dressed in that morning would no longer be our home. It had happened to me many times before. Countless numbers of my early writings, awards from school, and clothes were lost in our swift moves in the middle of the night. There were times we would go home and the locks on the door would be changed.

I can remember a Raggedy Ann doll I had for years that I left in a house that the locks were changed on while we were away. I cried for days about just going back for her. She was my friend. I had left her behind. I cried and cried until my grandpa grabbed me and said "it's just a damn doll, Tyierra! Shit, your mamma will get you another one just stop the damn crying over some damn fabric! It's gone!"

Not only did I carry everything with me when I was away from home with fear that I may never see the inside of that apartment again but also because there were times my things would come up missing. My grandfather would pawn them or sell them to people he met on the street, even my grandma would save receipts and take my things back. In the place of whatever item was missing was always a three-page letter explaining how it will help in paying the rent or getting the water back running; how my lost would help benefit the entire family. I would be promised something bigger, better, more expensive, shiner, something for letting the item go. The utilities would be back on, but within six or so weeks we would be homeless, hungry or without water again.

I grew tired of losing the things I treasured most so often. Packing my life in a bag and taking it with me was the only way to keep from crying about them later. Of course they would ask me for them after a search. I would lie and say they were lost or stolen instead of hiding in my book bag. I carried that habit with me into adulthood. Someone asked me in recent years why I was taking nearly my entire life with me to shop for groceries; laptop, iPod, phone, camera. I started to replay stories of the past in my head and realized I'm not in that situation anymore. That was the day I put my book bag down and broke myself of that habit of a childhood fear. I was twenty-three. However, there were times that I wasn't able to save the family with a shirt taken back to Walmart or the returning of a toy they never allowed me to remove from the wrapping. We just had to deal with having no lights, no water, or a home.

"Shhhhh," my grandfather glared at me while he turned the lights off in the kitchen. He placed his entire body on the floor next to my grandma. "Don't say nothing. The rent man is outside." Sounds of banging came from the front door. We listened, hearts pounding from our chest on the ground in the kitchen. I was only nearing twelve when I watched the moonlight sneak in the small kitchen window of the shotgun house. I stared outside at the duplex next to ours, or what we claimed to be ours. My grandfather hadn't paid the rent in almost four months and the owner was not very happy about it.

"Mr. Burnell I know you in there!" The man tried to look between the blinds. His silhouette danced in front of the windows. "I need my rent or you need to get out!"

By now the neighbors were surely either snooping, looking out doors and windows, or out on their porches watching the live action drama. This was not a new circumstance in this part of Uptown. We lived only a block away from what was once known as the Calliope Projects. With all the shooting and fighting around there, we were used to our cheeks kissing the ground.

I could see little critters feeling safe enough to come out in the darkness to feast on the greasy leftovers my grandmother had prepared. The floor was cold but the air was muggy. My grandfather was sweating and as always my grandma was praying that the rent man would just simply go poof and disappear. I wasn't sure what she really wanted to happen. Did she think she could just pray her problems away? Maybe she thought that a pile of money would just appear outside the front door for him to take and let us be. She was praying an impossible prayer.

As she finished her plea, we noticed that the banging had stopped. I thought to myself that maybe the worshiping of God had worked this time. My grandpa pushed himself up from the floor first. He crawled towards the living room. Grandma got up and then motioned for me to stand on my feet as well. I walked quietly over to my backpack to make sure everything of importance was still there. I had a feeling that even with us getting away with it that night, tomorrow was not promised.

As the zipper rounded my bag for my personal items, my grandpa screamed at me without coming above much more than a whisper, "Get down! He's still here!" The rent man had just pulled up again in his car. I wondered to myself where he had driven away to and why.

Shortly after being reacquainted with the ground, we could see flashing red and blue lights finding its way past the ripped blinds and into the house. My grandpa took a deep breath and stood to start towards the front door. He knew he had to face his fears one way or another. On his short walk to the door, another loud bang was made. This time it was two cops from the New Orleans Police Department with the landlord right next to them. My grandpa opened the door, slowly.

"Mr. Harris, we understand that you were told you need to vacate the premises. Is that true? Are you still here knowing you were to be gone by now?" A deep voice asked my grandfather. I crept closer to see what was happening. Both white officers were tall and thin wearing finely pressed uniforms with all the gadgets and gizmos on their belts shinny as if brand new. The lights from their car reflected off of their required equipment. One officer had a hand on his weapon and was surveying the space behind my grandfather while the other spoke. I peeped a little further around the large couch sitting in the living room. The officers finally spotted me. I tried to jerk back but was not fast enough.

My grandad turned to see me nervous and barely breathing. "Tyierra, come here," he called, "Don't be afraid. Police officers are here to help us not to hurt us." That was a different tone than what I had heard from mere days before but I dared no correct him.

I walked over to him as he glanced back over to the three gentlemen standing in wait of his next move. The lights were affecting my vision of our unwelcomed visitors. He wrapped his arms around me and had me face the officers and rent man.

"You gone put me out with my daughter? You gone put this baby out on the street for a few hundred dollars?" I could feel the passion in his voice. I could sense the tears about to stream down his face. He wanted those men to understand there was no other choices for him.

The rent man dropped his head and then closed his eyes. After taking in a deep breath, releasing it, and then putting his hands in his pocket, he spoke to my grandpa.

"Mr. Burnell. That is the same excuse you gave me for the last two months. It won't work again. Now, I'm sorry about the little girl. Really I am. I can give y'all a ride to a shelter if you want but I can't do this anymore. I got bills too Mr. Burnell. Y'all have to get out. I'm sorry."

He pushed me behind him and my grandma used her eyes to jester me to come to her safety. She looked disappointed but understanding. I couldn't save the family this time. The conversation continued outside with the officers, the owner of the house, and my grandad. Once back in with us, he explained to my grandmother that we could rest but that night would be our last night in that house. I had already seen that coming for our family, but it was nothing I could do.

The next day after the officers had disappeared and the rent man had departed home, I looked in my book bag to stare at my belongings. I could see my little worn out pink notebook with photos sticking out of some of the pages, a purple pen I had found at a bus stop, and a number of other random items. While I was happy I had some of the things that I cherished in a bag on my shoulder, what I really wanted was my home back.

We didn't go back that evening. The sofa in the living room, the tiny blue pinball machine I got the Christmas before, which I never got a chance to beat my uncle's high score, and nearly all of my clothes were left behind. "Let the rent man clean that shit up," my grandfather would say. He was happy with just the clothes he worn that day. He didn't know how badly it affected me.

We went to a motel in the east part of New Orleans after that. I can remember playing in the parking spaces and collecting beer bottle tops from the unpaved dirty lot. There was a nice woman who often used the same motel room over and over. I would get a quick smile and wave before she and her John would disappear behind a locked door. There were no other kids around. I spent a lot of time in the dirt right outside of the motel door alone and in my own thoughts. Not the best place for a child but anywhere is better than being face down on a dirty floor wondering what was going to happen to you next.

But there we were, once more face down on the ground hiding from something, wondering what the next moments would bring. It was a history lesson of my life. At least this time there was no rent man and I wasn't hiding my face from the mean kids at school. We were hiding from Katrina. Someone who we would have never imagined we would have to face outside of the normal landlord or police man who came to take us from our home. She was someone fresh to me but felt so familiar. This in a sense was nothing new.

I kept repeating in my head that a little bit of rain and some claps of thunder would not hurt who I am or change me. I knew I had been through far worst. If I could get through life with hopes a school lunch would fill me up and a backpack full of dreams, I knew I could manage a little storm.

# Chapter 7: Surviving with Strangers

*"Alone we can do so little, together we can do so much."*
**-Helen Keller**

It was dawn when I pulled my head up from my grandmother's lap and felt her hand slowly slide from my head. I wiped the slob from my cheek that had pooled as I slept. The dome was packed with people of all ages, races, and backgrounds hustling around. I never knew so many different people lived in New Orleans. I never really noticed how much culture was right in front of me until Katrina forced me to open my eyes. The hall was always moving and bustling along. Many people were passing us by but I didn't know to where. There was not much to do inside the dome.

My grandfather, who didn't sleep much that night after the water and wind came slapping at us, shared that the lights had "gone to shit" and he was sure we were running on backup power. I could notice now as the lighting was reduced and the cold air from the AC was no longer pushing out that freezing chill.

People were looking at each other confused and scared as I rubbed the sleep from my eyes. I could hear rumbles from radios playing back the memories of random survivors who were using their last little bit of charge on their phones to call the station and inform them of what was happening in their part of the city. I can even remember asking myself why they would waste it on a call to be on the radio.

News of what Miss Katrina had walked in and done to our home was rapidly spreading throughout the day from the radio broadcasts and from the new Superdome members who had found their way to the so called safe haven. One person told others around him he heard that some bridges were completely gone. I later found out that the twin bridges that connected Slidell and East New Orleans had been destroyed because of the rising water and that the bridge had damage to about 40% of the decks going in both directions. There was no way someone would be able to pass. Just another way to keep us trapped in the city limits.

It wasn't just that bridge that had taken a beating but the entire city of New Orleans. What was worst, NOLA was not the only place that was touched. The cruel Katrina had even changed the lives of those nearby cities like Ocean Springs, Mississippi after leaving an injured US 90 Bridge over the Biloxi Bay. A 13-ton oil rig from a Mobile shipyard escaped and ended up slammed against the Cochraine-Africatown Bridge. Seeing photos of the two objects tangled together some time later brought tears to my eyes and hurt to my heart.

Back in the Big Easy as people were being dropped into the dome, stories of looting was already wiretapping in. It was being seen in the walls of our shelter as well. The thirsty citizens of the city were breaking the glass of vending machines and searching the dome for supplies. Others were looking to turn a profit on the misfortune of what was happening outside of the arena. One young black man who didn't look a day over twenty was putting individual cigarettes in the air in order to find a buyer, "I got cigs for $5! I know y'all out 'bout now!" His stained white t-shirt barely touched the top of his sagging jeans that hindered him from walking without having to grab his belt.

As quickly as he had come he was gone, disappearing into a crowd of strangers. While people were looking for a quick financial come up inside the eight o'clock hour, the Industrial Canal levees that held Lake Pontchartrain back from the 9th ward, had breached. That meant our city, our homes, our every day as we know it was changing and there wasn't a damn thing we could do about it. I started to feel sick to my stomach hearing of the breech.

My grandfather could see that I was visually disgusted. He looked over to me and I stared back to him. His eyes were red and his hand dry from the lack of moister. His now dark blue polo style shirt that he had changed into had three buttons. He just blankly stared off for a few moments before turning his attention to my grandmother. She was quietly studying the words in her beat up burgundy colored Bible. I felt as if she was preparing for an exam at the end of the week that she was determined to pass.

Her focus never left the thin pages in front of her. Her pink lips motioned with the words she was reading. I couldn't find a single wrinkle on her and my grandma never wore makeup; not so much as lip balm. I did notice the salt and pepper hairs sticking from under the back of her short-styled wig. I couldn't remember the last time my grandmother wore her hair out let alone dyed it.

Her glasses she had bought from Walgreens a long while before were sitting on the bridge of her nose. Her big cheeks made me think of how Mrs. Klaus would have looked if she were real. My grandmother was such a beautiful woman.

I looked back to my granddad who had apparently been looking at me for a while. My pains from the storm had really started to affect me and he could see it.

"What's wrong with you?" he asked. His concerned tone was more jokingly then anything. I'm not sure he knew how to ask me if something was wrong. We never shared a real moment of concern.

I put my hand over my flat tummy and made a face full of ill, "I need to go to the bathroom."

We stood up and headed to the restroom which luckily wasn't too far away. My grandmother stayed behind to protect the few belongings we had and to keep claim of our spot. It was dark at the entrance to the ladies' room but I could hear other women talking. I glanced up to my grandfather and saw this confused yet concerned look as if to ask, "Are you going to be okay going in there alone" and I threw a look of confidence back to him.

As I walked in the restroom, it felt very muggy and humid. The air had stopped dancing around the bathroom. Two women who were in neighboring stalls were chatting to each other and it was easy to figure they came together as they spoke about soon going home.

"I can't wait to get out of here! I need to get to the house, get back to work. This shit playing with my green," stall number one stated.

Stall number two quickly agreed, "Girl who is you tellin'? Them kids gotta eat and who gone pay for it? This storm is just in the way!"

The conversation quickly faded as the two women exited their bathroom boxes and headed out the door. I was afraid in there alone for a moment but I had to go. I selected a stall that was close to the entry but didn't lock my door. I relieved myself but my stomach was still in pain. I used the dim light from what was creeping from the doors opening to look down in my underwear. And there she was... Aunt Flow. First Katrina and now Flow. In those few seconds, I was fed up with female visitors in my life.

My monthly cycle had decided to come and here I was without a pad in hand. I looked to my side and grabbed the end of the toilet tissue role and started layering it around my hand. This was a trick my grandmother had showed me when I was unable to afford feminine products in the past. When I finished turning my left hand into a mummy, I pulled it off and stuffed it in my underwear. I then repositioned my clothing. All I could do was hope nothing would get through. My cute Family Dollar baby blue skirt wouldn't be so cute anymore with a mishap. I decided that the next visit to the restroom I would put on a pad and change into some more period worthy clothing; black pants.

I quickly got back to my grandfather who was waiting outside of the restroom for me. He was picking at a scab on his hand and looking toward the floor. "Feel better?" He asked, "You were in there for a while."

I didn't want to tell him what was going on down below especially since he was already overly-informed about my cycle. When he thought my cycle was late, he would ferociously question and accuse me of an imaginary pregnancy. Which was crazy with me not being sexually active or any real freedom to even try and explore the possibility. There have been many conversations at the bus stop on my way to school that started and ended with "It's been about 25 days, so it better be here soon and you know what I'm talking about!" I couldn't do anything but stand in silence to avoid eye contact with those around us. I just decided I did not want to discuss it with Katrina's effects still knocking on our door. I quickly nodded to keep us moving.

My grandpa wanted to walk a little around the place to stretch our legs and get some fresh air. There wasn't much of it with the AC being out but it was better than sitting stagnate I suppose. We started a stride around the dome giving me another opportunity to analyze all the different kind of people that had made the Superdome their home. We walked for some time and I began to think we were lost, forgetting that the Superdome was a giant circle. People were trying to occupy themselves with making new friends out of strangers or even doodling on a piece of paper, but the same thought was going through all our minds; when are we going home, if there was a home to even go to?

My grandfather noticed someone he had known from the store he worked walking down the hall. I didn't personally recognize him or recall seeing him in the past. The two men stood there and spoke for a few moments.

People avoided bumping into them by walking around but it was very noticeable that people were growing annoyed with them standing in the middle of moving traffic.

"When did you get here?" My grandfather asked.

The man shook his head, "I been here as long as you have. And I'm ready to go. You can't put this many black people in a hot box and think it's gone be alright. I left my old lady at the house, I don't know where she at."

I turned my attention to the people around me again while my dad and his longtime customer continued their conversation. I twirled in a circle to see the full picture of those around me. Some even looked back. There were not many positive emotions from any of them.

I did wonder if anyone I knew was there. All those faces and I knew not one seemed ridiculous but it wasn't like I was a popular girl to begin with. It's possible I really may not have known a single soul there outside of the two hands I held coming in. That frightened me. I was alone there. The thought of what I would do if both of my grandparents died crossed my mind. It wasn't like I had a way out of there or even a place to run to if I did. I wouldn't know what to do, but who was to blame for my social butterfly wings not flapping?

I had always been the kid in the shadows. Only talking to kids that talked to me first. There were so many times in my past that kids and even in some cases adults rejected me, I quit on myself. I know I could be social. I was different but I was just like the other kids. I liked to play, have fun, and converse about random things. I needed to stop letting the people around me that I saw

95

every day be just strangers. I wasn't going to be the strange kid forever.

My grandad finished up his conversation and we started to walk again, soon making it back to my grandma who had been wondering if she should send out the National Guard to find us. He knew not to make her worry. Grandfather Burnell shook his head and told her to stop showing out. He said that as long as I was with him I was safe and she didn't need to show her ass by mentioning anything to those people in that dome. I remember him going on about letting people into our business and her sitting there with her mouth closed. Then I realized why I had to really back away from being social. It was because I had to always hide the truth about how I was living and it is easier to hide when you have few or no people around you. I knew I didn't want to continue like this for the rest of my life.

It was around noon when phone systems started to go offline and people could not reach others on their mobile devices anymore. I thought to myself about the storm being over and gone but even with the winds dying down and the eye of Katrina departure it was just beginning. The worst was not over. At 2pm the 17th Street levee confirmed to be breeched and the wound to the barrier would soon reach 200 feet helping to flood most of the city in less than a day. Close to four in the afternoon, the last barriers to be breeched, the two levees along the London Ave Canal, failed.

Unaware of the news of New Orleans falling to pieces, my family and I were sitting in wait. My grandmother was sitting against the wall with her head tilted back. It seemed like she had fallen asleep. Granddad was going through his old torn up wallet. The black leather like material was starting to flake and the window that showed his ID card was discolored. I sat in the corner looking out to everyone else while writing on scrap pieces of paper.

The young twenty something year old man who came before had reappeared still wearing the same shirt but this time there were cuts on one arm and bottles of water in the other. This time he had friends to back him.

"Who need water? I got bottles of water for $4!" The young man moved his swift feet across the floor to keep up with the other members of his water selling crew. A few people took the offer, which was more than his first trip through.

My grandfather and grandmother did not entertain the idea or the young man. They both just continued as they were. I'm not sure if they didn't want the water because it was from a stranger or if it was because they knew it was stolen. It's not like we hadn't indulged in something that was taken without being paid for before. Maybe it was the fact that he was a stranger. But were we really anymore? We all had one thing in common. We were all alone but we were alone together.

There were many strangers amongst us. Years after being in the dome I found that I was not the only person not being social. Doug Thornton, general manager of the Superdome since 1997, was with us and no one even knew. He was occupied, however, with other tasks. The Federal Emergency Management Agency, better known as FEMA, sent trucks to the dome to be used as temporary holding facilities for the dead. Thornton found it unfair to put the trucks that were expected to hold the dead right next to those trying to live so because of his words of disagreement the trucks were moved elsewhere.

By the end of the day thousands of people had made the Superdome home. Nearly 80% of the bowl-shaped city was under water, five-feet of that Katrina River was floating on Paydras Street right outside the Superdome mocking us. Katrina had even flooded out the National Guard's headquarters forcing them all to relocate their whole operation into the super structure. Katrina may have left us but she had not gone without leaving us lifetime memories of her visit.

# Chapter 8: Thou Shall Not Steal, Unless...

*"If I was gonna go to jail, I don't want to go to jail for stealing a bottle of water. I'll steal that $20 million. At least then it was worth it."*

**-Idris Elba**

I went to a superstore not too long ago to do some shopping. I didn't really get dressed up or anything fancy. I just threw on some navy sweat pants, put my hair up in a ponytail and took off. Not long after leaving my apartment I noticed the ponytail wasn't holding up all my hair on the sides like I planned for it to do. I usually throw a couple random bobby pins in there but in my rush to get to the store and on with my other errands, I forgot them.

As I was shopping, I found myself blowing my hair out of my face in order to drive my buggy around the other shoppers. Any woman will tell you, getting hair out of your face and keeping it out of their vision is annoying.

I was pushing the shopping cart down the aisles of the store when I happened to approach the sections that held all the hair care products. A pack of bobby pins caught my eye as if to be calling out for me. I only needed two to keep the hair up and out the way. I was not about to buy the whole pack when I had a million of those tiny things all over my bedroom floor. Plus, I had about six other places I needed to be that day and I found it unreasonable to keep scooping handfuls of frustrating hair out of my eyes every ten seconds. So, I did what I felt was justified. I took two of the hair pins, placed them where they needed to go in my mess of a head and carried on with my shopping for the afternoon.

Then it hit me, theft and shoplifting is just not in me! The entire car ride to my friend's apartment where I was being waited for, I was debating with myself on whether I wanted to turn around and tell the manager what wrongs I had done or if it would be easier to just call and ask for a supervisor. I needed to confess my sins!

The second I got over the threshold of my friend's place it was over. Three sets of ears heard me weep out: "I stole two bobby pins! I'm so sorry!" but of course they thought it was funny. They laughed at me all the way to the outlets to do our Christmas shopping. It was really serious to me though. I ended up buying the same pack of bobby pins that was luckily still there the next day. I didn't tell any of my associates I did, in fear they would tease me once more, but I felt better about myself.

My friends may have tormented me but they didn't understand at the time. They just didn't know what growing up in New Orleans surrounded by thieves and shoplifters was truly about. I can't recall how many times I've seen kids lose their brand new shoes to someone who stole them right from their feet, in the classroom nonetheless. I remember a robbery that happened right in front of eight other people in broad daylight while we waited for the bus to arrive.

To the thieves it wasn't necessary to work for their own shoes, cell phones, or lunch money when it was so much easier to take from those who were smaller and weaker. I've seen many times a mother who would rip open a pack of diapers and stuff them in their coats. While it had a purpose, it was still theft. Let's not forget the all too familiar story of the kid who steals a candy bar or Blowpop. That happened nearly every day in the store of an Asian family on the corner of Broad and Washington in the Uptown section of New Orleans. Stealing things wasn't uncommon where I grew up. In New Orleans, from the blocks I lived, you only had a hand full of options: sell drugs, be a shot girl or stripper on Bourbon Street, or steal. The worst case of stealing out of all I have seen comes right from my own granddad.

There were many situations my grandpa had taken things that weren't his. My grandmother even told me their love story of how they ended up leaving Texas fleeing to Los Angeles and it involved theft of a good grip of money out of a store's register. Most of the time it was to fuel his habit of horses but there were other times to make up for the mistakes he had made because of those horses. I saw the same events play out time and time again living with them. I just never thought I would one day be an accessory of his criminal acts.

My grandfather woke me up on a blistering night in the month of May. It was late; maybe one or two in the morning. My part of the world was fast asleep and there was no movement in our house. I looked up at him with one eye opened as he stood over me with an empty gallon milk jug and barely visible profile. The lights were turned off but I could tell it was my granddad. The moonlight hit his smooth skinned face just right and the lighting from the old box television was bouncing off of the right side of his body.

"Be quiet and don't wake up nobody," he whispered to me. "I need you to go next door and get some water."

The water had been shut off and all the sinks in the house were dry. My grandpa hadn't paid the water bill and the city had disconnected our supply only a few hours before. There was no warning and we weren't prepared. When I say we weren't prepared I mean we didn't do our normal routine when we figure out that the water will be shut off, which included running water in the tub and in all the sinks of the house along with storing a lot of it in storage containers and pots.

He wanted me to get out of my sticky spot on the couch which was my bed at the time and tap into the neighbor's water supply. I was barely awake when he told me to get up from my cozy slumber on the loveseat sofa and put on shoes. He descriptively told me exactly what he needed me to go outside of the house to do. It was strange for him to be tasking me with such a mission. I am sure he was able to do it but I was so much smaller and younger. I could go move around the house without being detected and if I were to get caught there isn't much they would do to a kid in the sixth grade pinching a gallon of water. The neighbors may even have pity on me.

My mind was all over the place. Wasn't this stealing? Don't people go to jail for stealing? I really just want to go back to bed or couch or whatever you want to call it. Even with my mind not fully wrapped around what was going on, I got up and slipped on a pair of shoes as he handed me the empty jug. There was no fighting my grandfather before sunrise. I was still kind of sleepy, he woke me from a dream I was having about my sixth grade graduation. Who would have thought that only mere days after putting my big girl school clothes on I would take on the career of a cat burglar.

We didn't live in a regular house like normal people. Anyone outside of my family would have considered it the basement. The way New Orleans homes are built, the "basement" is built above ground to prevent the underground rooms from being flooded. It was converted into a one-bedroom apartment and was a very uncomfortable place to live with my grandpa, uncle, uncle's wife, and their daughter who was born the December before. I slept on the couch and my grandpa slept on the other one which left no privacy for me. He had already told me many times before that I was too young for privacy anyway.

My uncle's small family slept in the bedroom that was separated by a wall the owners had built with old recycled paper if you ask me. My grandma had gone to California to spend time with her daughter, my aunt, Tressa, and wasn't aware of anything that was going on down south. Though she didn't know the water wasn't on in that late May, it was not the first the water was turned off. She had lived this life before. Grandma Ludie said she wanted to visit her daughter, but I believe she just wanted to get away from the struggle for a while.

My uncle Burnell and the rest of the gang were sleeping peacefully in their shared bed. I walked toward the front door. My heart, I remember clearly, was beating fast and butterflies flooded into my stomach. I could feel my chest moving from the overwhelming fear of being caught. My mind was telling me this was wrong but my feet kept moving. It was either get the water to flush the toilets or sit with the disgusting aroma of urine dancing around our noses.

"Turn off the lights before you open that door," he did that whisper that you knew if he was able to he would be screaming. Grandpa Burnell didn't want anyone to see a light shining which would draw attention to our house.

I glanced back at my grandpa. He didn't even look at me. He stared at the television as he sat on the edge of the couch that doubled as his bed. I guess he felt bad for sending me out to steal water from our neighbors. These were people we talked to every day who trusted us. I am sure they would just give us the water if we needed some that bad, but the embarrassment alone would have killed my grandfather. He knew it was wrong but what else was there for him to do at this point? In his mind, this was the only option he had.

I wrapped my hand around the doorknob and turned it to let myself out. It made a loud screeching sound that old houses seen in scary movies make. I took a deep breath in and stepped out onto the cracked concrete.

It was hot and muggy outside. That is the thing about New Orleans weather. When it's hot, it is really hot no matter if it is day or night. The moon gave light for me to know where I was going but the fear of the dark was still present. I closed the screen door slowly behind me, still with the jug in hand. Bit by bit, I creeped down the driveway into the neighbor's yard and then to the side of the house where they would usually attach their hose to the water spout.

I popped the top of the container that not too long ago held 2% milk and placed it under the faucet. I put a small amount in at first just to get the left over milk residue out so the water wouldn't taste funny.

It was quite strange and ghostlike that night. There were no cars passing on our residential street. I didn't hear not one dog bark or two cats fighting over a thrown away tuna can in the alley. I can't even remember if a cricket rubbed its little legs together to let me know it was there. It was dead silent.

My granddad's shirtless figure could be seen in the door. He was making sure he kept an eye on me and I wasn't going to be stolen. I think it was more of a lookout to guarantee no one caught me stealing water from the people who unfortunately lived next door to us. Him standing there or not didn't matter, I was still afraid.

It felt as though I was holding my breath the entire trip outside. This was really my life. There was always fear in me. It was always a lack of food, water, or housing for that matter, making me always afraid I wasn't going to make it through the night.

The jug filled and I turned the handle to stop the water. A little of it plopped in the mud creating a splash on my pants bottoms. I slipped back over to our door and quickly got into the house. I was relieved that it was over. Grandad grabbed the water filled jug from my hand ran to the bathroom, and began to pour it in the toilet. He had used the bathroom sometime before and now needed to flush. If you dump about a gallon of water in a toilet bowl, even without real running water, it will flush. You do have to dump it in at the right speed or you will otherwise have the bowl over flow, but it works nearly every time. My grandpa was a pro at the art of flushing toilets with no running water. We had to do it so often I couldn't see why he didn't already hold the official title of Flush Master.

After pouring all the water in the commode, he walks back to me and hands me the jug again. I look at the empty container as I reach out to grab it. I glanced up to Grandpa Burnell with eyes that begged him to not make me go. I could feel my throat getting dry; the same dry that you get when you are about to break down in tears. His reply was to look at me and say "You thirsty ain't you?"

I dead man walked to the front door and exited slowly, again. I walked over to the waterspout and turned it to release the water into the jug for a second time. As the liquid entered the jug once again, my eyes began to water. Maybe it had something to do with me being sleep deprived or maybe it was because I knew what I was doing was wrong. That was what I was taught my entire life; it was okay to take from others when you are in need something instead of being responsible and finding a way to fix the problem on your own.

Is this how life is supposed to be? Am I supposed to wake up in the middle the night and take things that don't belong to me? Is this a dream? Is this a movie? I just couldn't believe where I was. I didn't want to live like that, I didn't want to flush the toilet with the water from the faucet from people who taught me how to jump double dutch.

Back and forth I went, nonstop, in and out of the house filling everything I possibly could with water; from milk jugs to pots and pans. It seemed like it was hours I was doing this. The whole time fear filled my chest. What if the police pulled up and saw me doing this evil task? Would they take my granddaddy to jail? Would they take me to jail? Finally, my grandpa said that we had enough water to get us through the next few days and I could stop. I came inside and laid back down on the couch. I didn't go straight to sleep. Instead I lay there on my back staring up at the ceiling wondering what was the purpose of my life. While water is an important part of staying alive, why would my grandfather not provide that for his son, his daughter-in-law, and me?

While I laid there, staring into the open space, my grandad walked by several times moving the water from the floor near the entrance to the kitchen counter and the bathroom. I could see him looking at me out of the corner of my eye but I dared not turn my head towards him. I figured he would ask me what was wrong and I not be able to hold back any of my tears or my anger. He would tell me to suck it up and it was the way life is like always. It just wasn't something I wanted to hear. None of my classmates from school had to go through this; at least I didn't think they did. I just never understood why he would make me live this way. I wallowed in my sorrow a little while longer before I finally was able to drift back off to sleep.

The summer days soon began. It was hot, sticky, and the last summer before I entered middle school and in my own mind become a woman. I had grown so much in so little time. I slowly began to understand that my grandad had a problem more than a hobby. It was nearly the end of July, one of the happiest times of the year for New Orleans and we still had no water coming through the pipes of our home.

We were making it pretty much off bottled up water I got from the bathroom sink from my grandad's place of work when I went with him every day; of course he didn't trust me to stay at home alone. The rest of my water consumption came from me eating frozen cups made of Kool-Aid that one of the neighbors on our block sold for a quarter.

Every now and again I would ask one of the neighborhood kids to bring me out a cup of water to drink since we all were outside playing. It didn't look odd or out of place because we all were thirsty. My thirsty was just on another level entirely.

My granddad and I had just returned from the racetrack one afternoon and were walking down Louisiana Avenue Parkway on our way home when I saw a bunch of kids from our block outside playing in the street. I looked over to my grandfather and he already knew my question. He was in a good mood that day. He had won around $600 playing the ponies. It was not every day he came home with a profit.

"Go play with your friends. Don't go in nobody house," my grandfather walked into our home and closed the door behind him. I was over joyed to be out of his grasp even for a few moments.

As I hung out with the neighborhood youngsters, we all began to grow thirsty, as usual. I had asked the oldest of our group way too many times already for cups of water and I think she was getting a little suspicious.

"Let's go to the corner store and get a cold drink," one girl suggested.

"Yea," another girl agreed, "I want a pickle and hot chips. I ain't got no money though. I'ma go ask mamma for her change from making groceries today. I know she used some money because we used everything on our Louisiana purchase card last week." The girl got up and walked inside. I glanced over to my grandpa's door. I knew he wasn't going to give me any money to go to the store because he wasn't going to let me go to the store in the first place. I didn't want to stick out as the odd ball anymore, I was tired of it. "I'ma ask my grandpa if I can go," I said as I brushed off my pants and walked to the door.

I slowly opened the entrance to a cool and dark room. The TV was on some western movie. My grandfather was big on movies involving cowboys and indians. There he sat on the sofa with a coke on one side and a bag of Hersey's chocolate nuggets with almonds on the other. He had already removed his pants and shirt and was fast asleep with his hands resting on his over grown belly. I could see his body go up and down as he took deep breaths in, his chin nesting in his chest.

"Paw-Paw?" I barely spoke, "Are you awake?" Clearly I did not want a response but I thought I would try. I figured he was sleep and had no clothes on, it would take him a while to get up and peak out the door to see if I was around or not. I knew I could get away with going to the corner store and back. One more problem though, I had no money.

I looked over at my grandad once again. He was in such a deep sleep I knew this was my only chance. I could instantly feel the blood start racing to my face as I tried to hold back the tears with the thought that just crossed my mind. I glanced to the floor and saw his pants, with the belt still looped. I slithered over to his slacks and slowly dropped my foot on top of them. It felt as if a percussionist was using my heart as his snare drum. Faster and faster it went as I dragged his pants closer toward me. I never lifted my eyes from the site of my grandfather as I slowly bent down to riffle through his pockets.

I finally looked down to see what I was grabbing. I pushed back a few hundred-dollar bills and finally found a $20. I eyed up at my grandfather once more to confirm my decision before I took the single bill and placed it in my pocket. I pushed his pants back where I found them and swiftly but soundlessly I got out of there.

As I snuck to the store, I couldn't help but think how awful of a person I was. I had just stole! From my own granddad, I had just stolen money! With that thought in the back of my head I still proceeded anyway.

Once arriving at the store, I got myself an orange soda, bottle of water, pack of Now-and-Laters, and a pickle. I tried to stuff everything down my throat before getting back home so my granddad didn't question where I got the junk food or even worst where I got the money. I kept the candy tucked in my pockets as I walked home with the other girls from my street. As I bit off a nice juicy piece of my stolen money pickle, I knew I would never steal again. It tasted good in the moment, but I knew it was wrong. It just was not the life I wanted to live. However, I did enjoy finally getting something I wanted from him and him not being able to take it back even though it didn't feel right. It may have been a good pickle, but I realized stealing just doesn't come natural for me.

# Chapter 9: Wash, Brush, Floss, Flush

*"Once you wake up and smell the coffee, it's hard to go back to sleep."*
**-Fran Drescher**

The darkness came and went quickly. Hurricane Katrina was no longer a hurricane but a tropical storm as it danced over the state of Tennessee.

While the guests of the Superdome were hoping for their family, friends, and even complete strangers to be rescued from the flood waters, the NOPD were redirected from search and rescue missions to deal with looters instead. I've always mentally boxed with myself on which was worst: people using this tragedy as a come up for Jordan's and Gucci slippers or the police department being less concerned about the safety of the city's citizens and more focused on ensuring expensive merchandise isn't stolen. With lives at risk, should this really be the world's biggest concern?

My grandmother and I decided to go for a walk and find our family a meal. It wasn't like we had a choice of what we wanted. We had only two options; MRE or nothing.

Grandma noticed a line forming and assumed it was to food and water. There was no other reason for people to be gathering in lines at the moment, so this had to be to fill their bellies. We stood quiet for a while and absorbed what was all around us. People we had never met were quickly shuffling by and children were giggling not understanding completely the magnitude of being in the dome. The hall was dim, pulling energy only from the backup power, but I could still see the many faces clearly. Some people began breaking into groups by their race. I assumed it was for them to relate to each other and find that comfort that wasn't being provided anywhere else.

More followed our lead and started to gather behind us against a wall. A young black mother and son who looked tired and damp had formed directly behind us. The little boy didn't look much older than nine or ten. He was clinging to his mother's hip and she had a hand on his shoulder. His eyes slowly opened and closed fighting the battle of fatigue which he was clearly losing. The woman holding her son had obvious marks of fear but yet relief covering her face.

I could tell in my grandmother's eyes she wanted to say something. As much as my grandma talked, it was a surprise she couldn't find any words to speak. I saw the concern in her face as she kept looking back to the woman, then down to the child, and then over to me.

My granny must have seen the same anxiety I did on the young mom face. She turned around a couple times to smile at the lady and her son. By the third grin the female started to look towards the floor to avoid eye contact. But Grandma Ludie did not let that stop her from communicating.

"God is good! He got us some kind of shelter. Ain't He good?" My grandma's loud voice carried to the mom ears.

She swiftly responded with a head nod and a raised brow.

I could see the curiosity in my grandmother's eyes. The little boy was still grasping his mother when my grandma asked her how she ended up in the dome.

"Lines are getting longer around here. How long have you all been here?" Grandma asked.

"A few hours," the lady responded with distant eyes, "We were dropped off. It's a living hell out there. I never thought I would see the day." Her voice filled with a heavy New Orleans accent was low and crackly. Her tattoos were barely visible against her skin tone. Her hair untamed. Her blood colored eyes began to water. A few tears dropped to her shirt. The woman son eyes were now shut for good and he was clearly in a deep sleep even though his grip never let loose.

My grandma put her hand on the woman's shoulder and tried to tell her that it was God's will that needed to be done. The woman shook her head in disbelief that her God would let this happen.

"Naw, this is something else out there entirely. God don't do this. I don't care if he has to clean house he ain't gone clear it like this!" She realized her voice was getting louder as she glanced down to her son. "You were blessed enough to be in here when Katrina came rolling through. We were stuck out there! I had to pull my son out of a house filling with water and sit on a roof. We waited there for hours for help! Wet. God wouldn't do no shit like this!" She shook her head over and over not allowing my grandmother's words to touch her ears.

She continued her story to my Grandma Ludie on how she knew her 87-year-old neighbor couldn't have made it out. Trying to not be too loud, she leaned in closer to my grandmother to lessen the chance that her son would hear, "I don't know where his daddy is. He was at the house, then he was gone. It was all my fault. I knew he ain't have nowhere to go in this storm, but I told him he couldn't stay with me and it wasn't gonna be that bad. I thought he just wanted to use me again. I didn't want him to play with me no more and I done sent him to his death. God forgive me!"

The woman's single tears became streams. It was hard to watch her hurt. My grandma hugged her and insisted she knew what she was feeling. She even mentioned not knowing where her son, my Uncle Burnell, was. Even worst, he didn't know where we were. She was just as scared as the young mother was.

"But baby," my grandmother looked the twenty something woman in the eyes, "God got a plan. He not gone close a window without opening a door. You hear me? You just gotta be strong and look forward. Not just for you but for the baby boy you got to take care of."

I had seen my grandmother pass on the words of God so many times before to me, my granddad, a prostitute on the corner, a dog if it would sit still long enough to listen, but I had never seen her so strong in her words like this before. It was if this woman was put there to not only show how strong she could be but how strong my grandmother could be as well.

The line kept moving forward, slowly but moving nonetheless. The little boy was almost being dragged by his mother as she continued to talk to my grandma. Now the topic had switched from sending the father of her child to his death on to how he became her ex-boyfriend to begin with. A story I had no interest in listening to. Their voices soon became faint hums as I started to think where my uncle had ended. My thoughts soon turned into where my mother Yolanda was and if she had thought of me at all. She knew I was here in New Orleans. She had to have seen the news by now. I let the thoughts take me into a moment of depression.

What if I was still in that house?

Who would have cared?

Who would have known?

Would I even be missed if I were dead?

I didn't know how to feel. I never got that chance to have those feelings explained to me. I didn't know what those feelings were and why they hurt so much. Then I realized that those pains I felt included the cramps I was having and the lack of food in my stomach. Soon, I looked up and we were at the front of the line.

Between the both of us, we grabbed three MREs along with some room temperature bottles of water. My grandmother and I began to say our goodbyes to our line neighbors as the boy woke for his meal. Granny Ludie threw a quick "I'ma pray for you, baby" in as we started our walk back towards where my grandpa was waiting for us to return. We never saw the child or his mother again after our departure.

I wondered what was going through Grandpa Burnell's mind on our venture back. He could have been thinking about how maybe this was the end of the world as promised in the Bible. I quickly retracted that thought as the word of God promised he would never destroy the Earth again by flood, but then again was he cleaning the house of New Orleans like the lady had mentioned? He said never again would he destroy the entire world with a liquid squeeze around the earth's throat, but nothing in there mentioned the Crescent City.

When we got back to our home away from home, my grandfather was on the floor listening to the news from the sound waves provided by a neighbor. From what was being said there was not a lot going on during the moments we walked in on the broadcast. Just about a handful of people talking about the damages to the part of town they lived. Mostly the flood levels and how many fallen trees were blocking the roadways. There was no report on how many lives had been lost. Maybe they really had no idea. Then again maybe they didn't want to disclose what was really going on outside in those streets to keep the fear level low.

As I listened, I gobbled down my chow I was given without much chewing. I really didn't want to eat the strange meal in a bag but the hunger pains, I knew so well, were creeping up on me slowly. Before they became too much to handle I wanted to get them satisfied. All the food inside the MRE was new to me. I didn't think it would be that good. Looking at the plain brownish tan wrapping, it did not scream flavor but it was acceptable. It did the job it had set out to do. I then started to miss the stove and microwave. There is nothing like a bag of popcorn from an old box my grandfather would bring home from his work before having to force myself to watch a John Wayne movie with him. My grandma didn't enjoy what was inside hers at all. She spent a lot of time trying to get the food down. With every bite, she inhaled two gulps of water to wash the taste from her tongue.

She wasn't the best cook out there. Grandma didn't even drain the grease from the meat when we had ground beef. The tacos she made would come in a pool of orange grease that leaked from the corners of our Mexican dish. It was not much variety to our daily food choices. If I had to eat one more hot dog on a plain piece of sandwich bread or a plate full of pinto beans and rice, I can almost promise I would have lost my sanity. Thinking about what I could be eating helped me digest the brown bag meal a little easier.

Not long after discarding the brown bags of military deliciousness, Mother Nature called. If it wasn't enough that my cycle had appeared out of seemingly nowhere, now I had to relieve myself again in the dark from all the water I forced myself to drink. I tried to tell myself that I could make it just a few more days without going into that bathroom but I knew in the back of my head that I was going to bleed through more than I already had, even with my light cycle at the time. Having my dark pants on that I switched into a couple hours before, I was well aware if blood came through it would get noticed. I needed to go back into that restroom again. I had already tried to substitute a feminine hygiene product with rolled up toilet tissue that was not very reliable and I still hadn't brushed my teeth. I had to do something with myself. I knew what being the stinky girl was like. I was trying to avoid that yuck feeling.

I looked over to my grandma and told her that my bladder could no longer take the pain I had inflicted on it by holding in my urine. The fact that my teeth felt like fuzzy slippers in my mouth also was reason for her to escort me to the little ladies' room. I could see in her eyes she did not really want to go to the bathroom because she had just sat down but she didn't have no other choice. Letting me go alone was not an option. We searched through our bag to find a small face towel, our toothbrushes, and some toothpaste to share.

"Be careful going down there," my grandfather yelled over the radio at us as we walked away, "I heard the bathrooms have gotten pretty bad."

The bathroom was only one turn right from where we had made camp. The hallway was long and open. There were several different concession stands lining the passageway which were promised to be busy serving hungry and beer thirsty fans during the season. There were a couple of small vending machines on the side that the glass had been broken into. The restrooms on the corner had no doors for easier entrance, but this time it wouldn't be as easy as I hoped. The visit from before was rough without lights and no running water but this was unlike anything I had ever seen before. The bathroom's state had taken a dramatic fall from what it was just a few hours ago.

We were greeted by a wet floor at the threshold. There was some light coming in from the entrance but very little. The black in the room was overwhelming. There were a few faces the emerged from the darkness that displayed horror and disgust as they exited. The head shakes partnered with the covering of their mouths and noses as they gazed back behind them concerned me.

Are they smelling a dead body?

Oh my God there is a body in there I know it!

My mind wondered off to the worst possible outcome giving my heart a reason to start racing. It had to be some explanation for why there was not one but two FEMA provided trucks designed to be 18-wheeler sized refrigerators sitting out by the loading dock. They were morgues on wheels. Both trucks were quickly removed as it would have caused one hell of a news story but the thought that they had to do that is shocking.

My grandmother was close behind me as I continued my slow walk into the unknown. Her body kept pushing me forward into the darkness. I soon understood the woman's facial expressions. It was indeed a horrific aroma in the air but it wasn't a dead body. Those who created that tragedy were very much alive.

"What's that smell, God?" my Grandma Ludie asked.

"I don't know," I replied even though it wasn't addressed to me, "It smells disgusting. This is awful!"

I started to move quickly inside as I felt a thin layer of liquid splash under my feet. I figured if this was anything like swimming, I needed to just go ahead and jump in there, head first, to just get over the initial shock of the smell. Nothing would prepare me for what was about to attack my five senses. Walking in and looking at the back wall, it wasn't as dark as it was before. A backup light had managed to start working but was not as strong as it needed to be.

The smell, that had mixed with the upper 80-degree temperature, followed me to the side of the room the light was mounted. I looked in one of the stalls. Instantaneously I was sick to my stomach at what my eyes had found. Feces piled up in the commode. The smell was unbearable. Toilet water, urine, and traces of human defecation that had over flowed was covering the floor. It was surprising to see it all over one of the stall walls and soaking into some toilet tissue that had fallen on the floor. Others who had seen the same sight had thrown up their entire MRE at the stall door entrance right at my feet.

Right outside the stall swimming in the pale vomit was a couple of used needles that I nearly stepped on. I started to see more of them as I glanced around the dimly lit room. I knew in that moment I would never be a drug addict. To endure the smell for a high was out of the question. The restroom was pure chaos.

The next stall was just as awful as the one before. Maybe even worst. The next was just the same, and the next, and the next. What was worst, the hand washing stations were beginning to clog with toilet tissue after the women using them as urinals decided they still needed to clean themselves.

My grandmother and I decided to walk out and journey to the next restroom. We thought it would at least be a little cleaner. Maybe the cleaning crew just hadn't gotten to this bathroom just yet. Wishful thinking.

We got to the next ladies room and found it was even worst. We were greeted this time at the entry by a glass soda machine that had been recently broken in to.

Glass was covering the floor and blood covered the glass.

The familiar smells of feces filled the air as we walked through the entrance. My grandmother's face frowned up as she felt the splashing of water under her feet unsure of if it was water or some other God awful liquid substance. She covered her mouth to reduce the risk of gagging. I was not far behind her after glancing towards a faintly lit corner where someone had made their restroom on the floor. A pile of human dung sat in the middle of the tiles for all to view as it was crowned with the tissue used to remove the remains from the owner's backside.

While I stared around the room in awe of how much we had already degraded as a people, my grandma was looking for a decent stall. As the women continued to walk in and out, some not staying long enough to relieve themselves because of the smell while others just could no longer hold it, Grandma beckoned me into a stall that was "good enough."

I looked around the compartment as she closed the door behind me. A feeling of nausea filled the box. It seemed more like a horse stable than a restroom, forcing me to watch where I stepped. I turned around and pulled down my pants just low enough to release myself but avoiding the possible opportunity to drag the bottom of my pant leg. I squatted over the half full toilet and began to empty my bladder. I could hear the splashing into the commode on top of who knows what below me. The odd sounds were disturbing. I tried to close my eyes and drift off into another world while my body naturally was relieved.

My eyes jumped open and my heart dropped as I remembered I needed to replace my pad. I had only a couple left from the supply I brought from home before I was back to the home-made version of rolled up tissue. I looked around the small space to see some toilet paper dragged along the floor. I then turned to the wall to see just enough toilet tissue to clean myself for now and roll into my underwear until our next trip to the restroom.

I tended to the rest of my needs and exited the stall. My grandmother pinched her nose and went in after I told her to grab her own tissue since none was left. I stood guard in front of the door the same as she did for me. Once she came out she handed me my toothbrush from her purse. I looked down at the teeth cleaning utensil and then back at her. After taking a slow room pan of the level of disgust around us, I looked at my toothbrush with tissue wrapped around the head earlier in our stay at the dome and decided... no.

"Um," I looked at my granny with sad eyes and shook my head, "I can't. I'm sorry. This is too nasty."

She took the brush from my hand, "I don't blame you baby. I'm sure our bad breath isn't gone be as bad as this." She slipped the cleaning kit back into her bag as we headed out to my grandfather carefully tiptoeing around needles, floating fecal matter, and a flood of urine and tissue.

The day went on filled with new reports of what was really going on around us and the occasional rumor. Former President Bush decided to cut his month-long vacation short. He was nice and comfy in his Texas ranch before deciding that it was a good time to go back to

Washington the next day. Louisiana Governor Blanco was shocked to see the situation we all were facing on her visit but no quick response was given.

In the Superdome, security had a small jail cell in case of drunken disorder during one of the football games and it was filling fast with Katrina criminals. We heard gossips of a man being caught sexually assaulting a little girl. You could see some mothers pull their children close each time an unfamiliar face got too close. Rumor has it, an unnamed man jumped to his death from a balcony of the dome. Some witnesses claimed it was because he couldn't take the thought of having lost his family to Katrina, others said the situation reminded him of "the war" while some stories say he couldn't take being chained to the arena anymore. I was lucky enough not to have witness such an unfortunate event but I do remember hearing the screams of women as they saw his body fall from the air, unaware at the moment of what had happened.

There were very few trips to the bathroom after seeing its state. We eventually came up with the plan to just use an empty water bottle to spit our toothpaste remains into after brushing. To change out my tissue pad we did have to eventually go back into the filth of the bathroom but I didn't even go into a stall. My granny would find the cleanest spot to stand in the room and she would position in front of me blocking the view as I quickly switched the tissue. It wasn't the best option but anything was better than having to endure the toxic wasteland inside a stall.

# Chapter 10: Being Different is a Blessing Not a Curse

*"I always find beauty in things that are odd and imperfect - they are much more interesting."*
**-Marc Jacobs**

"Are you sure?" my grandma asked as she glared down at me. Her eyes were big and beginning to tear up. It was like she was watching the baby in me vanish. Her bob cut wig was a little twisted and her brown gloves weren't big enough for her hands. I could still see the dry skin of her palm.

I had a green and pink bubble jacket that we recently got from a thrift shop on Airline Highway. I was wearing my dark green plaid school uniform and had a nearly empty backpack on. I was only caring an assignment from school and a pencil my grandma had bought me from Walgreens. As I stared up at her and nodded my head yes, something in me told me I just had to do this.

"Okay," my grandma pointed to the dumpster right outside of our apartment complex. We walked closer to the smelly trashcan and she opened the lid. I caught a whiff of the remains of old garbage seeping free. I took one more look at it as it rested in my hands, half of the remains still swimming inside. I inhaled a deep breath right before I threw it towards the dumpster. I of course missed and my grandma picked it up and finished the job for me. No more baby bottle for me. I didn't want people to call me a baby anymore. It was time for me to grow up. I was seven.

As we got on the RTA public bus to head towards my school, I thought to what I had done. I had made a big girl decision. I was sick of that old bottle anyway. The nipple never stopped clogging with spoiled milk. Probably because I always fell asleep with it and my grandparents didn't wash it correctly. I remember hearing someone on TV the night before saying they were quitting the bottle cold turkey. Though they were talking more on the terms of vodka, I related it to my problem and decided maybe I should do the same. I heard a conversation between my grandparents about how my grandma was letting me get away with things that babies do a few days before. I had poured a box of grits into a 2-liter bottle of orange soda forcing it to spill all over the galley style kitchen floor and wasn't punished for it by her. Instead, I was to stand in front of my grandfather and drink the whole thing. My granddad forcing me to literally drink my weird mistake and me pushing myself off the bottle actually worked. I never drank from a baby bottle again. I was finally a big kid.

Besides being a big kid, I just wanted to be normal. I didn't see any of the other kids in my class ask for a bottle. It was just me and I was almost certain I was older than all of them, seeing that this was my second year in the 1st grade. I didn't get to take it to school. At that point the only time I had with my bottle was after class ended. My grandparents didn't care about the strange looks they got when I laid in their laps on our bus ride home with a baby bottle in my mouth. I didn't mind either for a while until I finally got a chance to be exposed to how cruel children really are in the New Orleans public school system in the spring of 1997.

It wasn't a year before that when I was asked if I even wanted to go to school. We were walking down General Taylor heading towards A.H. Wilson Elementary on General Pershing Street when my grandfather turned to me and looked into my eyes and said, "Once we get in here there is no turning back. You gonna be going to school from now on. You positive you want to start now or do you want to wait?"

Being seven of course I did. I wanted to play with all the other kids I saw going to school every day. I didn't know it at the time but I had lost a lot of social skill building opportunities already. I had missed pre-k, kindergarten, and most of the first grade year I was supposed to be a part of. It was already the end of March when someone at my grandpa's job pointed out "that little girl should be in school" as they watched me help him stock the shelves. Putting up the cereal boxes was my favorite part of our day together.

I didn't care that I couldn't spend the whole week with my grandparents anymore, I wanted to go to school. My grandpa tried to bribe me into changing my mind by throwing that tad bit of information in. He told me I would be at school alone and not with him or my grandma but my want never swayed. I wanted to go to school and make friends like all the kids on Barney and Sesame Street. So what if I couldn't read yet? That's what school was for. I was going to be the most popular kid in my class. I was going to be a somebody. I never knew how wrong I could be.

I looked up one day and I was standing at the chalk board in Ms. Bennett's 1st grade class. I was to connect one half of a word with another. Just draw a line from one side of the board to the other side. But I couldn't do it. I didn't know any of the words. I tried but I kept getting them wrong. My untreated eczema rashes on my right foot and under my nose were becoming really itchy. I didn't know I had a skin condition at the time but it was clear to the rest of the world. Going to the dentist was not common in my house either as my aunt got me my first cleaning at twelve. I didn't see the inside of another dentist office until years after that.

I rubbed the philtrum area on my face getting a bit of chalk on my top lip. Trying to rub it off only made my skin flake and I could feel the surface become warm. This wasn't unusual for me. My foot was the worst of all the rashes I had. It would itch so badly in my shoe, I would sooth the craving to scratch it by pulling my entire foot out and move my sock rough and hard against my red cracked skin. I would discover later when trying to take my sock off that it was now stuck to my foot due to the pus and blood drying during the day. I had a lot of yellowish red socks.

My teacher eventually came behind me and erased the lines I had created for me to try again, but I didn't want to. I wanted to go home. I could feel the eyes staring at the back of my uncombed head. At that moment I was the most popular kid in the school and I didn't want to be.

"She can't read!" a little voice behind me yelled. His words were quickly followed by a classroom full of laughter. I didn't bother to turn around when Ms. Bennett tried to calm the class. I felt like I wanted to cry. Our teacher helped me with finding the right answer by pointing to it on the board. It wouldn't be the last time. I could tell she knew I had no idea of anything that she was trying to teach me. I knew the letters but didn't know how to put them together to make the words. I could sense her emotion of feeling sorry for me. I hated that spot but it was only the beginning.

My lack of social skills had me do some really strange things looking back on my childhood. There was even a time I collected my chewed gum just to keep my time occupied. I tried to collect leaves but they died and my beer cap collection was thrown out by my grandma. Gum was the only thing I could keep.

I thought friends were made by just showing up and everyone would like me. I wanted to live in the life of perfect associates that never fought, shared secrets, and did each other's hair. Maybe a friend in my class could even help me with learning more words. I soon learned that life wasn't that easy.

There was a girl in my class, Kiara, who I wanted desperately to be my best friend. She was the pretty one in the class and so smart or at least compared to me she was. I would go home and play with my not so imaginary friend Kiara in the bathroom.

"You're my best friend Kiara. We are going to be friends forever!" Being a first grader that wasn't too strange but it wasn't enough. During recess, I followed Kiara and a couple of her real friends around the playground. I wasn't right behind her but it was not easily missed. The three would walk and make stops around the yard only to move seconds later when they saw me coming to join. It went on for a few weeks before Kiara turned around one day and crushed my little heart.

"Go away!" She turned and screamed before walking a few more steps. I thought it was directed at someone else; maybe someone behind me. It couldn't have been me because I was her friend. So I continued to trail her and her squad. She felt me still shadowing and turned once more. This time it was very clear who she was speaking to.

"Stop following me, Tyierra! You is ugly! You is stank! You can't be my friend! Your skin is crusty! So stop!" Her hands were up palm facing me and her neck rolled as she spoke. I couldn't believe she said it. I just stood there in the middle of the blacktop staring toward her as she walked away. Her two friends were filled with laughter along with a handful of other kids who had heard the confrontation. She glanced back at me a few times before disappearing on the side of the school. Her face carried anger in the eyes but joy in her smile.

*Crusty?*
*I smell bad?*
*Wait, I'm not pretty?*
*She doesn't want to be friends with me anymore?*

Little did I understand, she never was my friend. I didn't recognize the emotions I was feeling. I didn't know what shame and embarrassment was at the time but that absolutely was what I felt. I didn't follow her anymore after that, but it was not the end of my torment. That moment in the yard was the beginning of her mean streak for the rest of her life. For the remainder of the school year she teased me about everything nearly every day; my thrift store shoes, my not matching hair bows, me not being able to understand words. Everything. All because I didn't defend myself. And a lot of kids followed her lead. I was an easy target. The power she must have felt to turn me into something so different; a person that would now constantly question myself about who I truly was. I became the shy smelly girl in the corner. I was a nobody; the opposite of what I set out to be.

I tried to be independent by playing by myself but it didn't work. Playing on the monkey bars one day I was pushed off and told that it was no longer my turn. Falling to the ground I hit the wood chucks hard. They watched as I picked myself up. In anger, I kicked the tiny pieces of timber in the direction that they were playing. One of the larger boys hopped down after a few pieces I kicked reached him.

"Ain't no stank ugly ass girl gone kick dirt at me! EWWW! Look at her arms! She got ringworm! Oh dirty self!" he pushed me to the ground after noticing the cracked dry skin in my arm creases, being careful to avoid my rashes. The others laughed and pointed while others made faces at the thought of my dirtiness. I scraped my hands and the back of my legs. The kids dared me to cry. I didn't. I pulled myself up and ran off.

I didn't play much at recess after that. I would sit on the steps in the yard and count the ants traveling in a straight line to bring food back home. I remember thinking to the last ant to not follow too close because that ant in front of him was not his friend. I didn't bother telling my grandparents how I felt or what was going on in school. They weren't going to help me anyhow. They lied to me and told me I was cute in the first place. They could not be trusted. Not to mention they told me school wasn't a place I wanted to be. I hated for them to be right, but in those moments they were.

There were plenty of days I would find myself in the bathroom with the door shut crying. As an elementary school kid, that was the only bit of privacy I truly had. I'd sit on the closed toilet seat and ask myself, "Where did I come from?" I wasn't like my mother considering the little I knew about her and my grandparents did things the complete opposite of how I would think they would be done.

Maybe my father, my real father, was some amazing superhero that would one day come save me from this hell I called home. Maybe one day he would swoop in and take me back to a family that was ours and I would have a clan full of sisters and brothers, another mom, friends, uncles, aunts and maybe a dog. I never really was a cat person.

I would even have my own little twin size bed with soft pink sheets and a matching blanket. I would pretend to even smell the fresh shampoo scent from washing my hair that had rubbed off on my plush throw pillows. I would think about all my artwork and family photos covering my brightly painted walls and all the different books I had finished reading already piled neatly on a small shelf in the corner. I could imagine a little white desk right next to the window so I can see outside and know when all of my friends were coming to visit. I still can visualize their rainbow of bikes out on the front lawn beckoning me to come down stairs while my father pokes his head out the front door and yell for them to get off his grass. Maybe I would get to finally be normal. Then my grandmother would knock on the bathroom door and all of my dreams would fade.

My life was like this up until the day my grandpa and grandma were told that I would have to repeat the first grade right before summer break. It really wasn't a repeat. I wasn't there the entire year so I understood. My grandfather didn't.

"We not raising no damn dummy!" He said as he kneeled on one knee at the bus stop, "Is this what you going to school for? To fail out? To look like a damn fool? Fail again and see what happens!" Those words would scare me for years. I did not want to know what would happen. Every time I thought about giving up I would hear him yelling at me in front of all those people.

As I progressed in school things got a little better with avoiding being the center of attention. I began to become more aware of my surroundings and knew exactly what to say and not to say in front of others. It did not stop some people from teasing me for being the stinky kid in class but I got better at dodging trouble. And girls. I thought all women were evil for a long time. Between my mother, Kiara and a number of other women and girls around me who had done so many mean things, I didn't know who to trust. I didn't know how to make friends because I really didn't know what to look for.

I did get to finally make some acquaintances once I started my second round of the first grade. One of them being Shandrika Morris. Now Shandrika was a different kind of kid all together. Pretty, light skinned, brilliant, but mean as hell. She was a real Cajun girl with a heavy New Orleans accent and a lot of hood in her. How I got on her good side I do not know but I am glad I did. That was the first friend's house I got to visit, with the presents of my grandmother of course. There came a time that they needed someone to babysit me during a summer break and Shandrika's sister quickly volunteered. My grandparents' gambling and determination to not pay off their debts almost ruined my friendship. My grandma avoided paying Shandrika's big sister $20 for her services. Luckily, the family did not take their sums unpaid out on me and we remained friends. Even now we still communicate but you can bet they remind me of the $20 at every chance they get.

Even with the bond I built with Shandrika, I didn't truly learn the rules of what friendship really was. I carried over my lack of knowing better about friend boundaries into adulthood. I thought from my many encounters with kids being so cruel, that if a person is nice to me it means that they are a good person and someone who I could consider a friend, I was wrong. I met what I thought was a friend, Brittany, years later. With her, I would assume she was a faithful friend as she seemed to be there for me when I was always going through my hardest and toughest times but she was never really there fully for me, instead to benefit herself. Brittany took advantage of my desperation of not wanting to be alone, but I let her, so it to was my fault. I just wanted friends or family so bad I let her rob me of my time, money, and energy.

I avoided making other serious connections with people around me and potential lovers to satisfy her connection of loyalty, so I thought. She would constantly have something negative to say about who I dated and once even told her mom I was neglecting her and not coming around a lot because I was in a committed relationship. I felt bad and thought that maybe she was right, and that I was really being a bad friend for not giving her all of my time. I didn't need to make any other friends anyway as she had a couple she brought with her that I knew were my friends as well too, right? When I finally woke up and really understood the situation I had put myself in, I gave her a heads up that I was seeking to move out when the lease was up on our apartment to buy a house for my son, my dog Mushu, and myself. With this news, I never thought she would get angry at the idea of me wanting better for myself until I was informed by someone else that she was very disturbed with the thoughts of me not wanting to keep providing for her and move her with me. All the things I had shared with her over the years had been shared with a complete stranger to try and belittle me due to the jealousy of my success.

I honestly thought a friend would have been more excited and proud to see me want to own a house at such a young age. I just couldn't believe I was getting the news of my own life story from someone I barely even knew. I finally did what I felt necessary, kicked her out of my home. With her went the two friends I thought would still remain close to me. They did not. Truth was, she was telling them the same thing she told anyone who would listen, how she was helping me a lot more than I helped her and that I had put her in a state of depression. She never paid a single bill outside of her own acquired debt and barely helped put food in the house. I literally took on the responsibility of keeping a roof over all our heads because I thought that's what a friend should do if the other wasn't able to financially.

Her two associates still probably think the worst of me for removing this woman from my home along with her young daughter, in which she would later express she gave birth to in order to keep me webbed in her lies. Brittany had a child to make me feel bad if I ever wanted to break off our friendship. Yes, literally went out and found a random guy from a dating site to make a child with to keep me in bondage to our camaraderie. She knew I would never want to turn my back on her and her baby, seeing that she was the only one there for me in my time of need when I had my son. While I was thankful that she volunteered to assist me, I later realized that she would use this situation to make me feel as if I was indebted to her forever. She treated our friendship as if we were married. If I knew it was all just a ploy to ultimately benefit her, I would have ended the friendship years ago but I didn't know any better. I never knew that the moments you learn to make a connection with people as a child would really affect how you would do the same as an adult. I put too much trust in her, and just people in general as an adult hoping to make friends and keep them, that I ended up damaging myself.

I learned about how connections with friends truly work throughout my life not only from Shandrika and

Brittany but at least one other woman. It was when I reached my 8th grade year at McMain Secondary school in Uptown New Orleans that I met her, Terrian Marchand. While no one's life is perfect, Shandrika's seemed as if it was; she had a sister and brother, friends, one roach and rat free solid house, and two parents who loved her dearly. It felt like home there. I wanted her life. I wanted to be Shandrika.

Terrian, however, was me and I was her. She lived in the projects with a single mother and had a little brother. She had been teased about just about everything you could think someone could be teased about. Her hair, her clothes, even the environment she grew up in. She sounded a lot like me and I resembled her. She was physically built a lot different. I was tall, light skinned, and slender. At times I was so skinny I could see my bones and I was still sporting my eczema on my face, arms and toes. Terrian was the opposite being about half of a foot shorter, more on the heavy side, and a creamy chocolate complexion. Her hair was dark brown and coarse. While mine was also stiff it was more of a dirty red. We were two peas in a pod and only a hurricane could rip us apart.

I remember telling her I was friends with some of the members of the boy band group called B2K while on the yard of McMain to gain her interest in talking to me. I loved the popular heart throbs and so did she.

"You know B2K?!" she screamed. She took a large white binder from my hands that I had created with every B2K magazine cover and article I could find. A lot of it was printed from school computers and old magazines no one wanted. I even would write my own articles with information I would find online. There I was being the odd kid again but I felt comfort in scrapbooking magazine pages about Omarion, J-Boog, Lil' Fizz and Raz-B with glue and tape I borrowed from school. I still scrapbook to this day.

"Yea! Me and Lil' Fizz go way back! In fact, he owes me for a bag of skittles I bought him the last time I was in Cali!" Of course I didn't know them but in my head I did. It was one of the few things that kept me sane. Pretending to know a famous group of popular, cute, and talented boys who would be proud to call me their friend felt... normal.

"Really?" she asked "He's my favorite! Oh the kisses I would give to that man! You just don't know!" Terrian clutched my book and stumped her feet. I could see the passion she had for that man was just as strong as mine. I continued my plot of Lil' Fizz and I being just friends, but he possibly wanted more. She even asked me to hook them up. I told her I would see what I could do.

As she flipped the pages of the book she would move in excitement. Her smile was huge and gorgeous. I could tell she knew the stories I was telling wasn't the complete truth but her imagination was as bright as mine. As I watched her jump around, up and down, a group of kids walked by behind her. The mixed crowd of boys and girls looked over at Terrian in her enthusiasm. One kid spoke just loud enough for Terrian and me to hear.

"Look at her yellow arm pit stains. Ewww! I bet she smells!" He was referring to the blemishes that had formed in the pits of her shirt arms from excess sweating.

Her face was stunned and if her skin tone was a little lighter her cheeks would have been bright red. She knew it was there but I'm sure she didn't expect it to be said out loud in front of friends but Terrian kept on pushing and kept her cool. She ignored their harsh words and their quiet giggles and kept going. She just continued her conversation with me, "So about this Omarion. How long have you known him?"

She didn't let what other people said about her affect her progress in life. She had been through so much in her short time already that words on a few sheets of paper really could not explain it all. I looked up to her. Even after hearing it continue throughout our time at McMain, she never moved away from her bright smile. I idolized her strength. It was not long after we became close that I found out why words from some nappy head little kids did not affect her. She had other issues she was dealing with inside that I will never be able to replicate.

"What's wrong, Terrian?" I clutched my new articles about our favorite boy group in my hand. I was planning on showing her what I had found on J-Boog a few hours before on the internet. I thought she had failed a test or someone had really said something to hurt her feelings but it was something much worst.

"I was raped," the words I could not comprehend. My brain did not fully understand how to deal with what she had just told me.

My first instinct was to ask by who. She quickly responded with her mother's ex-boyfriend who no longer lived in their home. It had happened whenever the boyfriend and her mom were still dating. A million thoughts started to run through my head. I didn't know why she would tell me, but I would find out later it was because she had grown to trust me. When she demanded for me not to tell any of the adults who could process this information better than I could, I felt stuck.

She hadn't really accepted it to be true yet. She was dealing with this battle with herself, by herself. I didn't want to share what she told me because I didn't want to shatter the trust she had in me that allowed her to share the nightmare with me in the first place, but I could not bare to see her suffer. Every day I looked at Terrian after that for about two weeks, I saw her pain. She would cover it with a smile or a quick hilarious fantasy about a marriage with a B2K member, but I still sensed it. Her telling me was her reaching for someone to talk to. As a friend, I only thought it was right to find her the help she needed. I told the school guidance counselor.

I honestly felt a bit of relief soaked in disloyalty. I wanted her to speak with someone better than myself but I knew our friendship was over. When I found out Terrian and her mother were called into the school to speak about what was shared with me, I felt I had lost a friend, but in reality I hadn't. I felt a little distance between Terrian and I for a few days but it didn't last long. She later would tell me that she was initially embarrassed when she found out I had shared it with the school counselor. She felt as if she was wearing a sign across her chest assuming the entire school knew, but she wasn't angry. She knew I wasn't trying to hurt her. I hadn't lost my friend after all.

She communicated to me that her mom was shocked but accepted her, something she thought before would not happen. Her mother even asked if Terrian wanted to press charges, but Terrian's faith in God's wrath decided against it. She did admit that her relationship with her mother was a bit different after that because her mother too was dealing with her own internal demons but they both continued to build a stronger bond with each other.

Terrian bloomed into a beautiful woman and has become a success, which is a rare occurrence for an average hood rat in the Crescent City. She has earned a second bachelor's degree in hospitality management and tourism with a concentration in culinary arts and now travels the world gaining experience in creole culture and food styles to bring home to the states. She still is my hero.

After meeting Terrian, I began to truly love myself. I thought me being different was wrong. But it wasn't. Before, I could only remember negative memories. Kids, girls and boys alike, were so cruel and for the smallest things. Even in adulthood, it was clear I let the wrong people in my life. But now I look back and think of how much none of what people made me out to be mattered. I don't want to be like everyone else. No, I wasn't cute, I wasn't smart, I wasn't the best dressed, I didn't have a lot of friends but my loyalty sometimes was given to the wrong people anyway, and I honestly did smell at times but my life could have been worst. I could have been worst. People who know nothing of me do not define my actions. Terrian is the best example of living above your past. If she can be strong, if difference made her the rock she is today, what is holding me back from doing the same?

Now I remind myself at every opportunity: This day is a new day. Yesterday does not shape me and tomorrow has not yet arrived. I will be the best version of myself today. I don't know everything but I know enough to be my own most dangerous weapon. I'm not perfect but I will walk as if I am. Beauty is not all that defines me but I still consider myself music to the eyes. I will not let others determine my happiness or who I will become. Loving someone else first means loving myself. Let no one come before me. I am my own circumstance. I am my own role model. I own who I am. I will create my legacy.

# Chapter 11: A Little Rage Never Hurt Nobody

*"People won't have time for you if you are always angry or complaining."*
**-Stephen Hawking**

It was already September 1$^{st}$ when I looked up and realized it was Thursday. I had seen and heard so much already and it hadn't been a week, yet it felt like a month of pure hell. The day before, food in the dome had started to come up short. As more and more people were coming in, the supplies grew thin. The heat had gotten wicked. I was sweating, as was my grandparents. My grandfather usually kept to himself, but this heat was making him drowsy and he was not fully with us anymore. This was not a state I had seen him in previously.

He wasn't the only person who was broiling in the world largest sauna. As I laid on the floor using a couple pairs of pants as a head rest, I could see men walking around in the 90 degrees plus with no shirts on and women stripped down to their bras. The heat mixed with the smell of thawed freezers, destroyed restrooms, mold growing in the air vents, and thousands of bathless bodies rubbing together was a toxic concoction of disgusting.

I too was burning up but I didn't even think about suggesting to my grandparents that I take my shirt off. My face was on fire and I was visually overheated colored in red. I could feel the balls of sweat rolling into my armpit. At the time the deodorant I was allowed to use, Teen Spirit and Lady Speed Stick, was not working at all. I felt filthy. Between my period, the heat, and the useless cheap deodorant, I was a walking pool of funk. However, I was not alone unlike the times before in life when I was the stinky kid in the back of the class. I just wanted to take a bath but that didn't seem to be in our future anytime soon.

Many people were being left unattended for so long around us. Elderly women just sitting without communication with others, some children even left to fend for themselves while their juvenile mothers went to scavenge for water and food. How could they? How could they feel it was okay to leave their kids just sitting there knowing what kind of people were walking around in here? Maybe they felt safe leaving them thinking the village would watch over them. Somehow I knew it was only because they had to.

There were so many rumors. I could hear the tales starting to grow. One voice would say they saw a little girl getting raped in the filth of a restroom. Another would say they heard of someone who got shot. Some of the words I knew stemmed from some kind of truth but of what, I was unsure. Unlike my grandmother who was very interested in the Superdome breaking news from the gossiping old ladies near us, I tried to remain distant from all of it. It was way too humid to further frustrate myself. Besides, it was a lot to accept as truth. As one of my favorite poets, Edgar Allan Poe, understood, "Believe nothing you hear, and only one half that you see."

There was one story of a shooting of a national guardsman that was partially true. The night before while on patrol through a flooded locker room in the dark, a National Guardsman was jumped and hit by his attacker with a metal rod. He ended up shooting himself during the confrontation in the leg probably in a panic. A little different from the story we heard of someone stealing his gun and taking their shot at attempted murder.

After that incident, I truly saw the Superdome as our prison. Barbed wire was put up around the dome in various areas to protect the Guardsman. It was like we were sentenced to some kind of punishment for being citizens of New Orleans. I was growing annoyed and angry. I wanted to do something about it. I wanted to get up, march over to whoever was in charge of that mess and honestly slap them clean across the face for the hell that we were being dragged through.

There was an episode of Dr. Phil some time ago where a little boy, Noah, was angry at his mother Wendy for disciplining him. He told her to shut up and when she didn't he went off and slapped her right across her face. Everyone watching, including the mother, was astonished that it happened. No one would expect me to do it. No one would imagine me walking up to someone in uniform and backhanding them. Just like they did not expect Noah. That's exactly how I wanted them all to react. Just shut up and listen! But instead of getting up, I let the heat become my penitentiary chains. The heat, the smell, and the hunger kept me weak; kept us all weak.

The day before, on August 31st, so much had happened. My grandpa and I started our day by gazing out to the field only to be forced to look up. Gaping holes of light so charitably provided by Ms. Katrina shined down on the field like spotlights. The field was trashed and soaking from the water that snuck through the roof. It did not look anything like it did on Sunday afternoons during the season. It was an entirely different place altogether.

While we were looking at the holes in the roof, Louisiana Governor, Kathleen Blanco finally ordered a complete evacuation of the city of New Orleans. Luckily, the city of Houston and their governor Rick Perry opened the Astrodome to Katrina evacuees even though we did not know it right away.

Former President Bush, while aboard Air Force One on his way to Washington DC, flew over New Orleans to survey the damage that Katrina had made in her visit. This is something he would later regret doing as many, including myself, would accuse him of being disconnected from the tragedy below him. In 2010, he even admitted that letting the photographer take that legendary photo of him looking out of his safe plane above the disaster was a big no-no. I would agree, that it was.

Once Bush reached his destination, he spoke in the White House Rose Garden on the search and rescue teams that had been deployed in the New Orleans area as well as FEMA's plan to send buses to move the Superdome residents to Houston's safety.

This news came right on time as the same afternoon, the levels of water had equalized between the Crescent

City and the 40 miles long 25 miles wide Lake Pontchartrain. In the mist of everything else, the teams of rescuers were trying to save those who were unable to save themselves from attics and rooftops but there were breaks in communication, that is if there was any communication at all.

Then in rolled September. There was a good bit of positive that was created the day before but it may not have been enough. The morning began with claims from former President Bush that he did not anticipate the levees would crumble.

However, former FEMA Director Michael Brown would tell CNN a couple years later that Bush was fully aware of the possibilities of a breech. It is still hard to believe, to this day, whether or not Bush fully understood what a breech meant as it is difficult to know if Brown was telling the truth. This was the same man who told the entire world that he had just found out about NOLA evacuees being stuck at the convention center but later reviled he knew prior to September 1st.

Rescue operations, by both boat and helo, were halted as rumors of gunshots at emergency helicopters had spread but were not true. There was one individual who was arrested for shooting in the air as a helicopter passed but it was in the days after. So many more lives could have been spared if that did not happen.

As I laid there in thought of if my grandparents would survive this or if even I would make it out, I heard it. The mayor's voice. His deep accent was streaming over the radio air waves in full force and holding nothing back. He was telling the world what was really going on in the city and what the public facing government was hiding behind the country's back, right next to the crossed fingers voiding their promises to fix Katrina's mess.

The mayor started speaking on how they wanted to use local public school bus drivers to get the people of New Orleans out. But this situation obviously was pass the level of local drivers.

"They're thinking small, man," the former mayor expressed to the radio personality, "And this is a major, major, major deal. And I can't emphasize it enough, man."

Even though he was correct and it was far beyond calling up school bus drivers to help get us out of there, it would later be questioned on why Phil Coale's aerial photo of countless school buses that could have gotten people out of the city to safety prior to the hurricane weren't utilized. Why was there such poor planning? Maybe because the country didn't care about a city that made great king cakes, threw beads, but unfortunately also housed a large percentage of black residents.

The radio reporter continued asking questions to the steaming mayor, "Do you believe that the president is seeing this, holding a news conference on it but can't do anything until Kathleen Blanco requested him to do it? And do you know whether or not she has made that request?"

"I have no idea what they're doing," Nagin responded, "But I will tell you this: You know, God is looking down on all this, and if they are not doing everything in their power to save people, they are going to pay the price. Because every day that we delay, people are dying and they're dying by the hundreds, I'm willing to bet you."

The Superdome citizens looked around at each other. Dying by the hundreds? What do you mean dying by the hundreds? Just how many people were left out there and how many people was this country willing to let perish? Our jaws were dropped and hearts over flowing with fear. Former Mayor Nagin was letting everything flow out; he was blaming the majority of the deaths on the ears that did not listen to him. He tried to explain pumping stations were going to go underwater, endangering the lives of sewage and water board workers. That meant no way to get water out of the city.

"And what happened when that pumping station went down, the water started flowing again in the city, and it starting getting to levels that probably killed more people," as Nagin spoke the hall got quiet. Quieter than it has been since first setting up camp there days before. I remember thinking they were going to let us die in the Superdome. It was a trap.

My grandfather's taste in locations for us to live in the city was not always ideal. It wasn't the best, having to stick tissue in your ears to avoid having roaches crawl in them as you sleep. There was even a location we lived right off of Canal Street that lodged a mature colony of termites that showed off their wings. I later read that male and female termites are produced with wings so that they can reproduce and the wings fall off after mating. During the time we lived in the swarm, I had to wrap myself in two sheets and pray they wouldn't crawl under and attack, even though termites aren't known to bite people. I still could hear them flying around and even land on top of my thin sheet layers of protection.

The worst was in East New Orleans, living in an apartment with my grandparents while having nasty, filthy rats. I'd say more like mice but in my mind at the time they were big, diseased rats that chewed holes in walls and could bite me! My grandfather tried to get rid of our rodent problem by placing these sticky glue traps that looked like a sheet of paper down in different spots of the house. They did catch a few of the mice, and some roaches too. It was so sad, you could hear the mice squeaking for help. My grandparents would just take the trap outside and through it in the dumpster.

There was one day I, for lack of anything else better to do, was running around in the living room of our apartment and found my foot stuck to one of the glue traps. Luckily, it was not the foot with my bad rash and there were no mice previously dying on the sticky paper. I yelled for my grandma to come pull it off as it was really scaring me. There were other bugs on the trap that were still alive and had begun to wiggle for freedom, one of which I could feel moving directly under my foot. With all the commotion of me yelling and the trap being waved around in the air as I laid on my back kicking my foot toward the sky, I guess the tiny roaches thought they should try to escape. It seemed like forever before my grandmother reached me. She found me about to die, in my mind at least, and my face covered in tears.

"Don't throw me out!" I yelled to her.

"What?" Grandma Ludie closed her eyes finally understanding what I was trying to say "Tyierra, I am not throwing my baby away. We throw rats in the trash

150

because that is where they belong. You just got stuck in their trap that's all. I can take it off and it will be over. Now hold still."

That same feeling came over me sitting there listening to the mayor. I was confined in a trap that was meant for the rats of New Orleans. They did this on purpose. This dome was put here on purpose to just kill us all and throw our bodies in a dumpster! I believed I was no longer a kid or even a human to society. I was a rat.

The mayor went on about how the city of New Orleans needs martial law, something I didn't fully understand at the time. He expressed to his interviewer how the city was out of control because of looters. Some were really taking advantage of the situation but others were trying to survive. He also was asked about his opinion on the rules of having to allow people to help us and how he felt about those of authority that did not request aid soon enough.

His next words I believe opened the eyes of a lot of people. "Well, did the tsunami victims request? Did it go through a formal process to request?" He even went on to talk about the events of September 11th and how the president was given supreme powers to assist the people of New York City. "Now, you mean to tell me that a place where most of your oil is coming through, a place that is so unique when you mention New Orleans anywhere around the world, everybody's eyes light up, you mean to tell me that a place where you probably have thousands of people that have died and thousands more that are dying every day, that we can't figure out a way to authorize the resources that we need?"

The Mayor was audibly pissed. He demanded that press conferences stop and real action take place. Then he spoke the words I vividly remember, "Now get off your asses and do something, and let's fix the biggest goddamn crisis in the history of this country!"

"He's a damn fool!" my grandfather yelled out, "He is not going to raise his negro voice at those white people and think he gone get away with it! They gone hang his black ass for that!" My grandfather did not see any good coming out of the interview because he was a black man from New Orleans. Who was going to listen? I did. Everyone around me heard his words and I know someone with a tie and a salary in Washington DC heard him too. It was time to stop being political and be realistic and sympathetic.

Not only could you hear the anger in his voice but the desire for his New Orleans family to be whole again. His words moved every ear that heard him. The passion behind him reviling his knowledge of how every moment lives were being lost and people being stuck in and on their roofs with water up to their neck brought more dropped jaws and even more tears. He finished the interview by admitting that New Orleans would never be the same after Katrina and he was right.

But I sometimes ask myself, was the former Mayor Nagin really concerned with the welfare of his New Orleans people or was he too busy in his own affairs? Or was my grandpa right and they "found" something to hang him with? I personally think it was a little bit of both._In early 2014, Former Mayor Nagin was found guilty on 20 of 21 charges to included bribery and wire fraud. He took more than $200,000 in bribes in which some were related to contractors seeking work to rebuild after Hurricane Katrina. Now, his passion and longing for a better future for New Orleans residents has no meaning and is of no value to the city's survivors. He was a crook and he was the face of all of us. He is the rat problem that we did not want. He once was known as a mayor that used his anger and his position to help bandage some of New Orleans but now he's also recognized as inmate 32751-034.

# Chapter 12: A Creole Woman? Crazy!

*"I don't usually lose my temper, but if I get angry, it's true - I'm scary."*
**-Eva Mendes**

"Dominique La Rue? Now where did she get that French name?" Redd Foxx's character Bennie in one of my favorite movies, Harlem Nights, asked.

Quick, who was Eddie Murphy's character, responded, "She's Creole."

In surprise, Bennie replied to warn and show concern, "Oh well you don't wanna mess around with one of those Creole women. You'll fuck around and get a root put on your ass."

"What's a root?" Quick asked.

"It's like a voodoo curse. All them Creole girls know how to do it."

No we do not. I always get asked if I know some spells and if I would teach them. I'll often get the draw back and a shove as no one wants to deal with a Creole woman from Louisiana because we are all crazy. My favorite question is if I have a voodoo doll tucked in my purse on standby. I do not know how to do voodoo or hoodoo, which is folk magic, and no I have never owned a voodoo doll. I haven't even liked dolls since loosing my Raggedy Ann.

Yes, we have all heard of the red brick dust sprinkled at the front door to keep evil out. Even the myth that we New Orleans women use voodoo magic and our "red gravy" in sauces to put a hex on men to force them to love us and stay forever. I don't know a single woman who has done that. What you fall in love with is the friendliness and warm feeling a Creole woman gives off when she's happy, not her sauce. With that being said, what I do know is Creole woman are a bit crazy sometimes. It has to be something in the water in New Orleans because anything can set a NOLA woman off. It could be something as serious as infidelity or something as small as a burger.

My Uncle Burnell, who I refer to as Juney or even my brother, met Chinetha Lakeisha Porter while she was boarding a bus on Canal Street in the downtown part of the city. Chinetha, also known as Nikki, was 19 and barely over five feet tall; 100 pounds soaking wet. She was the pinnacle of the Creole beauty of New Orleans with her smooth skin and heavy accent. Her long nails and high hair always gave her away as a southerner, if the two golden teeth didn't do it first.

It was truly a sweet story between my then 20-year-old uncle and Nikki. This pretty petite woman and my rough around the edges uncle made the perfect twosome. The Crescent City in 1997 would gladly have elected them as the cutest couple. They were the perfect young and free pair. Then she got his name tattooed on her arm and got pregnant.

Having a tiny baby boy named Burnell Harris III around was amazing. I felt like I had more family. Not only did I have a cute little cousin to play with but also an extended clan through Nikki. But there were times even with them I didn't feel accepted. Ms. Deb, Nikki's mom, I never felt really liked me. I was the weird kid and so different. There was a moment when I was eight when she asked me to tie Baby Burnell's shoe as he sat in his walker. I couldn't do it because I didn't know how. She gave me this look I would never forget. I know she thought I was slow. She just knew there was something wrong with me.

I will admit she wasn't my favorite either. She was so mean to me. I really didn't like how she laughed either. She would cover her face with her hand when she giggled because she was ashamed of the missing teeth in the front of her mouth. I guess I didn't help our relationship as I once slammed Nikki's hand in a car door accidently, as she had a habit of holding the outside of the car when her window was down. I can still see Chinetha wiggling in the front seat to try to get free. Ms. Deb never truly accepted me around after that.

Not long after their son was born, Juney and Nikki grew apart, I'm sure it had something to do with the behavior of my uncle but it really could have been anything.

He has always had a way with women; the wrong way. Juney really did drive Nikki to her crazy point sometimes. While I was in the fourth grade, Chinetha came busting in the house my grandparents and I stayed in at the time. My uncle lived only a few houses down the road but wasn't at home and my grandfather was at work.

"Ms. Ludie!" Nikki yelled waving her hands in the air, "Yo' son is a pain in the ass and I can't stand him!"

My grandma tried to calm her down with her soothing voice and a plead of mercy for her son, "Baby, you don't mean that y'all love each other. Don't do him like that. Y'all got a son. Be nice."

"I ain't trying to hear none of that Ms. Ludie!" Nikki headed for the door as she rocked her head back and forth with her eyes closed, "You okay, but your son really ain't shit! One day he gone make me kill his ass! I'm tired of playin' games with him!" Her small voice was putting out big boy words. She really was a boiling pot full of frustration and fury. I never thought it would really take place. I knew women in New Orleans were irrational and sometimes a bit senseless, but nothing like that would happen.

Living in New Orleans, you learn a lot about its rich culture and history. Madame Delphine LaLaurie, a name you may find familiar because of the American Horror Story (AHS): Coven season, was a real live holder of more than fifty African American slaves who once roamed the New Orleans French Quarter streets. Yes, she was a real person. She was a gorgeous depiction of the upper class; throwing extravagant parties and eating off impressive china in her three-story home at 1140 Rue Royale. Behind her splendor and riches was the evil that many people think all Creole women have.

One of Madame LaLaurie's slaves once while brushing her owners' hair hit a snag and infuriated the Madame. As the slave girl tried to escape from another awful whip lashing, she fell from the top of the home to her death. Madame was caught treating her slaves so bad she was forced to give nearly ten of them up. Members of her family ended up buying the slaves, however, and giving them back. During a house fire, apparently set by one of the slaves in order to escape Madame LaLaurie's cruel behavior, investigators found she had starved some of her slaves, put iron collars around their neck, along with a number of other God awful things. They found one slave woman without her arms and with pulled off skin in attempts to make her look like a caterpillar. Delphine LaLaurie, on the other hand was more concerned with her furs and jewels. Now people see the ghost of the slaves on the streets of New Orleans with their mouths sewed together and their eyes scooped out. Or at least that's how the story goes.

My favorite, Marie Catherine Laveau, a voodoo queen and another name you may know from AHS, lived only a couple blocks away in the French Quarter with her pet snake Zombi. Laveau worked as a hairdresser for white and wealthy families. Some say Marie Laveau gained her powers gossiping with her clients or she would get her information from customers at a brothel she had not too far away. I, on the other hand, believe the tale of her getting information on her clienteles from their slaves by intimidating them, then using the information to impress their owners. She was also a Creole woman but didn't use her power for evil but instead to bring joy.

Laveau's is buried at the St. Louis Cemetery. It is said that if you visit her grave, some believe to be housed in the most haunted cemetery in America, you will see people have placed their X's on her grave site. This is from those who have returned to show gratitude to Marie Catherine Laveau for giving them a wish they desired. Marie Laveau is a positive face of voodoo and a positive face on the Creole culture. Nikki, was not. As beautiful as she carried herself, she was a ball of sizzling angry air.

There are plenty of women like Madame Delphine LaLaurie who had no reason to be evil but was anyway. You could literally give them the world and it would not be enough. Then there are the Laveaus of the city. Marie Catherine Laveau was a woman who supposedly had powers that would completely change lives but used them only for good. On the other hand, no one questioned her abilities to avoid meeting the punishment of a shrunken head. Lots of woman in New Orleans are just that way. The crazy doesn't come out unless you make it come out.

My uncle got involved with a radio dispatcher at a cab company he was driving for to make ends meet while still participating in and off and on relationship with Nikki. Juney admitted to using the dispatcher for her services and money as she really was not his type. Juney is more into small petite black women. Instead of just breaking it off, he was breaking her heart. Her name was White Heather.

One day, who knows when, White Heather and Nikki got in contact with each other. Supposedly, White Heather stole Juney's phone as he was sleeping, copied down some of his contacts and called the numbers. The lucky number she called first was none other than his baby mamma. Nikki then also called another young lady once her and White Heather had befriended, or in Juney's words manipulated, Nikki. This was probably in order to form a "Burnell Harris Jr. Must Die" cult much like the movie about the poor soul name John Tucker. The young woman's name that they tried to contact was Black Heather.

Black Heather was confronted by Nikki and White Heather and after denying the acceptance into their posse, was promptly cussed out over the phone for being involved with their man. Being from New Orleans, an angry confrontation didn't scare anyone, but words from Chinetha Lakeisha Porter were not just words, or even threats, they were promises.

Early one spring morning in 2002 when the street in front of my grandfather's basement house was quiet, Juney was slumbering. My uncle had moved out of his house and into his father's one bedroom to save a little bit of cash. Next to him laid Black Heather. No other soul was at home. The house was still. Fast asleep and surely worn out from the night before, they napped in peace as the only sounds that were being heard was the soft chirps of birdies outside the bedroom window greeting the sun.

Then there was the sound of Nikki and White Heather's twisting in the lock, a stolen key to let themselves in. All at once, the quiet was broken.

"Burnell! Help!" Black Heather yelled as her nude body was snatched off of the queen size mattress by the tiny fist of Nikki. Chinetha's hands were filled with the surprised woman's expensive extensions. Black Heather's screams woke my uncle and pulled him to his feet.

"What the fuck are y'all doing!" he yelled at the women still half asleep, "Let her go, Chinetha!"

"No Burnell! People tired of you and this shit you put them through!" Nikki continued to beat the girl in the face while also relieving her of her weave; throwing each removed track to the floor. White Heather attempted to attack Burnell but was unsuccessful. Juney detached the white woman from him by tossing her to the floor and all while having no clothes on began to save the beaten woman from the wrath that was Nikki. White Heather continued to smash on the woman with her partner in crime. With more pushing, screams, crying and slamming, Juney was finally able to get rid of the women from the brutally beaten girl's body. Tears streaming down her cheeks, Black Heather was finally freed. The two home invaders fled out the same way they had came and bolted to White Heather's truck. Juney jumped into a pair of pants, to not make the situation worst running to the street naked, and out the door he went.

"You crazy white bitch!" He picked up a large rock from the street and threw it at the moving black truck as it backed up to speed off down Louisiana Avenue Parkway, "Both y'all fuckin' crazy!" The rock cracked the glass of the truck further pissing the white woman off.

After calling the NOPD to report the break in and fight, more like a savage attack, Juney would face charges himself in Jefferson Parish for vandalizing the woman's vehicle. They would quickly be dropped as of course they did not stand up against the criminal acts of the women. Both Nikki and White Heather would be charged with battery in Orleans Parish for the assault on Black Heather. My uncle soon after got a restraining order on the "crazy white woman."

It wouldn't be the last time my uncle ran into some trouble with the womenfolk of New Orleans. His now ex-wife Dujan would later pull a chef knife on him for a similar situation in the exact same house. The craziest part of the whole story is, he still to this day, years after the fight, after the charges, restraining order and divorce he communicates with all of them; Black Heather, White Heather, and Dujan. It must be the red sauce.

Nikki sadly is no longer here with us. Her life ended on June 6, 2011. Chinetha was born with heart complications and it was a miracle she lived passed the age of five. After suffering a heart attack, she was removed from life support. It was only done to avoid serious brain damage and life in a persistent vegetative state at East Jefferson Hospital in Metairie, LA. She was 32. Her heart couldn't take the stresses of this world anymore. While she was an angry little thing, she was an irreplaceable woman who is truthfully missed.

I was not short on anger myself. Growing up as I did I was very much introverted and a withdrawn girl who was easily taken advantage of. When I finally landed on my own two feet, however, that changed. I didn't want people to take me lightly anymore. I demanded respect and if you didn't give me that respect, there would be hell to pay.

In late 2010, in Virginia Beach, VA I was having my usual conversation on the phone with my grandma.

"How is pop doing, since he won't get on the phone," My grandpa refused to talk on the phone at the time for whatever reason and I had to inquire on his health status through his partner.

"He's doing alright. In the front room watching TV. How are you doing, baby? You need anything?" Her concern for me, I now am sure was a concern for herself.

She was lonely but also full of fear for me being so far from her protection.

"I'm fine woman," I replied, "Just hungry. I'm on my way to get a burger."

As I drove to the fast food drive thru, my grandma started to go on and on about a church she was going to now around the corner from my old elementary school that she had visited years before. She was so happy to be in the house of the Lord again and getting to praise him for keeping her alive one more day. I was happy she was enjoying being back in New Orleans after all of what had happen. While I did miss her and my grandpa, I was pleased I did not have to deal with them anymore. I felt free and independent. I was my own woman and nobody was going to stop me from being me.

During all of my day dreaming of liberation, I didn't notice the line to the speaker of the drive thru had moved.

"May I take your order?" a loud voice came through the intercom.

I glanced at the menu even though I already knew what I wanted, "Uhh, yea can I get a..."

"One moment, please!" The same voice shouted. I thought of how impolite that was.

My grandma was still on the phone with me as she heard the offensive woman scream.

"Where are you at, Tyierra?"

"Getting something to eat. This woman, I tell you what," I shook my head as I waited for her to come back to get my request.

"Okay go ahead with your order," finally I was on my way to a full belly.

"Can I get a number two, with a Sprite and a large fry?"

"We don't have no Sprite?" I could not tell if she was eating on something or maybe chewing gum but her smacking was distracting.

*They don't have Sprite? Who runs out of Sprite?*

"Okay, Dr. Pepper?" I asked graciously.

"Our soda machine is down. We got water, juice and tea."

"Why didn't you say that at... tea please," I held my frustration with the worker in to avoid confrontation. I could sense my grandmother knew I was heated at the employee as she too took in a deep breath and slowly released.

"Is that it?" The voice from the speaker growled. Without even responding I pulled my black Mitsubishi Galant up to the service window. Of course the first window had no one working there so I had to proceed to the second booth of the building and provide payment for my order. The fast food worker handed me a receipt and closed the sliding window without a single word. All I could think of was if her manager knew she was chewing gum like a cow while dealing with the customers and how unclean my food must be noticing her extended blue nails as she gave me my debit card back.

I could hear my grandmother continuing a conversation around her wanting to buy a-new-to-her piano from a thrift store. "It's real nice, Tyierra," I could hear her smile through the phone, "Almost like brand new. You just wait until God bless me with that first-hand pickup truck; no miles on it. First thing I'm going to do is get me that piano right on the back." I wobbled my head knowing secretly she would never get that magic pickup that she wanted to fall from the sky.

I just decided to go along with it to keep her pleased, "That's good. I hope you get it. You gone drive pop crazy when you do."

"That man ain't gone block my blessings," her voice began to catch a serious tone. She went on about how my grandpa was the reason she was missing her blessings from above in the first place. I didn't get to hear the long list of why she felt he was blocking her blessings, as I began to wonder what was taking so long for my order to come. Three women were just standing there laughing and carrying on. The young lady with the headset even glanced over to me, stopped laughing, and then turned her back in my direction.

"Rude! I know that cow did not," I blurted out.

"Who is rude?" my grandma asked in the middle of her sentence.

"Nobody. Don't worry about it."

They were in no rush to provide me my order. Soon enough, a lady different from the one who collected my payment stuck her arm out of the window with a paper sack holding my food. The bag was wrinkle and the worker wasn't look at me as she extended it to my car.

"Here."

"Here?" I asked.

"You ordered a large number two with a sweet tea?"

"Yes!"

"Here."

My face was visually and physically hot. I could feel the smoke coming out of my ears. I took the bag from the bad-mannered woman.

"My drink?"

She rolled her eyes, as if it were my fault I didn't get my drink, let the window slammed, beckoned for her co-worker to bring my tea, and handed it to me in silence. I drove off in anger.

With my grandmother still on the phone. I began my drive back home to my small apartment only a stop light and a right turn away from the fast food burger stand. After parking in one of the assigned spots, I grabbed my belongings and walked to my front door. Getting inside my grandmother continued her words and I tried to forget the attitude of the fast foot worker. Grandma Ludie spoke on the city and how she was ready to leave despite being in a good church but Burnell, my grandfather, was not. She thought it was because he wanted to stay in NOLA for some crazy woman who lived around the corner. I flipped on my TV and sat on the sofa and opened my bag to a straight path of rage.

I unwrapped the noisy paper of my sandwich and took a big bite. It was still cold. Like ice cold. Like still frozen cold! How was it even possible for this burger to be still frozen? I dropped my burger in disgust.

"Ewww!" I screamed.

"What? What is wrong?" my grandmother started to panic "What happened? Are you inside?"

"I'm fine!" I replied, "My burger though! It's freezing cold!" The burger wasn't even what made me angry. I wrapped it up and threw it back in the bag right next to my fries that were getting colder by the second. I reached in after to get my straw to wash the thought and taste of raw icy cow swimming around in my mouth out. I moved the freezer burger. Then the fry box. Then the napkins. But there was no straw! "Oh my God! No straw? They couldn't even put a damn straw in the bag!"

"Tyierra! It's just a straw!" my grandma tried to calm me but I was seeing red.

"It's not the straw! It's everything! And I am hungry! They never do anything right!"

Against my grandmother's better wishes, I jumped back into my car speeding back off to the restaurant. I don't even remember the words and prayers she tried to make me hear as I was too busy trying to drift through the cars to get back to the burger joint. Once I arrived, I parked right in front of the building, grabbed my food and proof of purchase and stormed through the door.

I told my grandma to hold on, slipped her in my pocket and proceed to act an ass at the front counter. I threw the bitten burger in front of a manager. The small remains splattered out of its wrapping and all over the counter. I demanded a new meal that was properly prepared.

"Also new fries! My damn fries are cold now because I had to come back up here! Y'all act like I want to come in here and act a fool! You must like it! Just do yo' damn jobs hell! It don't take too much brain power to get this job done! But no! People gotta act stupid for you to do right!"

I felt my neck dancing around to try and further prove a point. The lady apologized, fed up with my ranting, refunded my money and got me a new order. The entire store, customers and workers alike, had their eyes on me. I snatched a straw out of its holder and walked out of the establishment mumbling under my breath.

*I did that! I made them do what I wanted them to do. I got the respect I was suppose to get the first time! I* was like years of being treated like less of a person had just came out on that counter as the burger spattered down. I had been angry before, even around my grandparents, but nothing like that.

I sat down in my car and started to eat my fries; my nice, fresh, just dropped fries. When my pocket began to ring again.

"Tyierra!" my grandma yelled through the phone, "What is wrong with you? I've never seen you act like that! Next time stay home and make your own food and you wouldn't have to act like that! What if they would called the police? What if something would happened to you? I can't help you all the way in that Virginia if I am in New Orleans!"

I just shrugged my shoulders and tried to explain to her that it wasn't the burger it was the principle. I had spent my money on something and I was demanding the respect that came along with my medium fry.

For the next week my grandmother called me once a day and asked if I had cooked something to eat or if I was going to any other restaurants causing a scene. The answer was always no to both questions. I knew her calls and questions were all out of love and concern. She was right for the most part. I shouldn't have behaved as I did. It was a lot worst then I described. I even felt bad in the days after.

On Saturday, October 2$^{nd}$, 2011 my grandmother's name flashed across the screen of my phone. I picked it up after rolling my eyes as I was sure she was going to ask me again if I was eating at home or if fast food was my main source of my diet. When I answered the phone, my grandmother's voice told me she had sent me $30 to buy myself a loaf of bread and ground beef to make my own burgers.

"That should be enough for a bag of fries and some cheese, too. You should be able to pick it up at Wal-Mart," she added.

I closed my eyes and smiled. That woman always found a way to try to shield me. I knew she was concerned, I shouldn't have done it in front of her, really at all. And here she was. Giving me a portion of her fixed income. "Thank you. You didn't need to do that. I don't need it."

"Well, keep it anyway. I just want to make sure my baby got something in the house to feed herself. I'll talk to you later. I need to walk up here to get me something to wear for church tomorrow. I love you, baby."

"I love you too," I ended the call.

That was the last time I got to hear my grandmother's voice. She passed returning home that evening from getting something to wear for church due to congestive heart failure. It was only six months after we all found she had breast cancer, a secret she had kept from us for years. She was 57.

For a very long time I blamed myself for part of her passing. My anger, my Creole character, may have put her to the edge of her life. My stress of being away from her was enough. I learned in the days after her moving on from this life that anger will get me nowhere. No one respects it, they may fear, but they will never respect an angry voice. Think about it really, which is more valued? Being angry is normal but it should be expressed with hesitation. Anger made me feel I lost a piece of myself; a piece I will never be able to get back. I try each day to be kind, to help people understand, and to attempt to keep the Creole in me under control.

Not to be confused, don't take my kindness for weakness. I'm patient but I have learned to protect myself when I need to. Just try not to get my order wrong or I may have to pull out my voodoo doll and magic spells.

# Chapter 13: "We Gone Take Care of Y'all"

*"Religion that is contained only within a church building is a weekend hobby, not a personal faith"*
**-James Lankford**

*Hey God-*

*I don't even feel right praying. Getting on my knees and talking to someone I can't see has never been my thing. I don't know if it's because I'm not sure if you will listen or if you are even real. My mamma told me to come to you. She said you can make this go away. I don't know. I just don't see how. According to her you saw all this coming anyway. You are "all seeing." She said if you blink the world would pretty much be done. She told me you don't sleep. She told me you watching me right now. I don't know if it's true but if it is, it's kind of messed up. I think you closed your eyes on us. Now everyone around me is begging you to show them how to get out of this but what we not even understanding is why you even put us in this? I thought you were going to always protect them and wipe away all the tears and pick us up when our feet hurt and make sure we have food and clothes and make sure we have somewhere to live. But I know you better than I know anybody else. They asking you for guidance but I already know you can't guide us out of anything because you not even looking.*

I rested next to my grandma writing a prayer to God in my journal as she read from her Bible. Just a few moments before, she had told me that prayer changes things; something she always would say. I was sitting in my frenzied and heavy feelings. I had prayed. She had prayed. My grandpa had prayed. Yet, there we sat. I was told that God may not come when you want him to but He is an on time God. In my head he was way past fashionably late.

He was too late for the countless people who could be heard in the attics of their flood homes by rescue workers. He was too late for the little girl who was torn away from her mother's arms in the powerful current of the flood waters. He was too late for the families who were going to be affected by their missing loved one's casket that had floated out into the Mississippi. He was too late for some twenty thousand people at the convention center and the seven lives that were lost there. He was too late.

My faith and belief in God had always been on the fence. It sounds stupid but I really could not truly believe. What higher being would put his creations through what we were experiencing just to test our faith? That's kind of mean. It's kind of being a bit of a bully. Church was my number one biggest pet peeve. Not because of how long it was or that my grandmother

172

wanted to go nearly every day of the week when she did go. I actually loved to go to church to get the message. I felt freed hearing the words from the Bible from the minister. Even the choirs would get me excited to be there. It was mostly because of how my grandmother let it take over who she was or who she could be. It was the people sitting in the pews that boiled my blood. How could it be a church of God with all of this hate, evil, and unacceptance floating around? Worst of all how could it be a holy place if it was only a place my grandmother lost her meaning?

My grandma would spend her last few dollars on a nice church suit to wear on Sunday to avoid the judgement of her sisters in Christ. I've seen her spend hundreds on new wigs and church clothes combined and not think about paying a bill first. It never failed. She would come home after church on Sunday complaining to my grandpa in front of me on how she needed a new church home. She believed that the devil was there. So she would stop going. We would go to another church for a few months, she would find a way to attend nearly every day no matter if it was Bible study or choir rehearsal. Everything she would earn working part time at a local Winn-Dixie would go straight to hair, church outfits, tithes and offering, the building fund that nearly every church had, and the occasional lotto tickets. Grandma Ludie would then feel the first lady of the church was jealous of her connection with God or the male choir director and then just stop going again. It was a never ending cycle.

In between churches my grandma would keep up her lotto ticket purchases. She would put her tickets in various places in her Bible, wishing and hoping that those numbers hit the following night. She put her entire life in the hands of an invisible man in the sky.

"God gone take care of us, baby. He gone touch somebody heart at that light company and they gone turn our lights back on."

Certainly did not occur.

"We gone get that five-bedroom house if we keep praying about it."

Never happened.

"Just pray for food and it will come."

That did not work either.

"If we praise Him he gone show us the way." This one was her favorite saying but it drove my grandpa crazy. She would be up at three in the morning banging on a toy piano keyboard she bought from Family Dollar singing church hymns and preaching to her undetectable audience behind two boxes draped with a Navy blue sheet. When my grandpa was fed up with her praises he would yell to the room demanding silence. It never worked out in his favor. She only got louder rebuking him in the name of the Holy Spirit. "Get out of here Satan!" is all that could be heard in the house after he tried to end her service early.

My faith was really tested when I found out that she did not want to go to the doctor after being diagnosed with breast cancer. She hid it from us for years before my Uncle Burnell saw the effects of it not being properly treated through her shirt. He had noticed puss covering her white blouse and then found red and purple cysts all over her swollen left breast. It looked like a rotten tomato; something third world.

What did she say though when she was forced to go to the doctor and they told her it was already too late but her chances would be better if she got the breast removed?

"I'm gone be alright. God not gonna take me. He gone see me through this and I am going to live to see Him come in the clouds of glory."

I was pissed. Seeing my rib, the only positive thing in my life, lay in a New Orleans hospital bed knowing she was pretty much just giving up killed me a little inside. Seeing the frustration in my face and the tears pooling in my eyes she turned to me when the room was empty.

"You okay, Tyierra?" her concern for me made me even more angry.

"No." I looked down to the floor as I sat in the chair in the corner. "You passing up the chance to live because of what? Because God? God isn't going take it away like a magic trick! You gone have to put in some effort! Faith without work is dead. Isn't that wat your Bible says? Is he telling you to do nothing? I doubt it!"

"I'm scared, Tyierra," her head dropped and her eyes closed.

I walked over to her bedside. I could see her swollen red breast through her gown. It was bulging out further than the other. As my eyes began to water I grabbed her hand, "I am, too. I can't believe I am saying this but He wouldn't put more on us than we could bare, right? Then trust in Him and do what you think he planned for you to do."

I soon left the room to find my grandfather. Since they weren't married, the doctor had asked him to leave while he talked to me about her health. I found him waiting in the hall. I stopped my grandpa from going back into the room and then questioned him about truly believing in God. He said he believed in God but was not as concerned with the church as Grandma Ludie. I told him how my faith wasn't there. I didn't mention to him why. I didn't want him to know I had just told my grandma to have faith but I was putting on an act. Somehow I am sure he knew.

"She gone learn the hard way. Tyierra, I heard of this man who went fishing and ended up in a storm that caused the boat to turn over," He started to share a story.

I looked puzzled at him not understanding what any of it had to do with this situation.

"Hold on let me finish. He went fishing, the boat turned over in a storm. He started praying. 'God, if you can hear me, please help me out of this mess I done got myself in.' The man prayed and prayed. While he was praying, a big boat came by and tried to throw him a rope but he just yelled back up to the boat crew, 'Thank you but God is going to save me.' The boat kept going and the man kept praying. Sometime later another boat came by. Again the man said 'Thank you but God is going to save me.' The boat kept going and the man kept praying. Then the man died and ended up in Heaven. He got a chance to walk up to God and ask Him, 'Why? Why, God? Why did you leave me out there to drown and not save me?' You know what God told him? God said 'You fool. I sent you two boats.'" He began to chuckle and I followed.

"That man is Ludie. She has to see a literal miracle to believe. It's not always going to be a neon sign pointing to that miracle but she just doesn't understand that. God gives us common sense. Well, most of us. You can be that boat in her life. I can. The doctors can, too. But in the end, she has to make the choice on her own to grab the rope. You've done all you could." He was right.

She ultimately listened and got her breast removed. It was only a temporary fix as she died a little more then six months later. Even up to her dying day, that woman was faithful to God. She of course didn't live by every verse in the Bible but she did plenty to show her loyalty. Maybe she didn't get on that boat in time.

As we sat on the dome floor waiting, I just kept thinking about all the times I asked God to help me before. I knew my letters would go unheard. He wasn't listening to me or worst he was, and still wasn't doing anything about my requests. Maybe it was because I didn't believe and my faith was false. Maybe his eyes truly were closed.

My grandma turned to me, "What you writing about?"

I closed my journal, "God," I replied as I started to sit more erect, "I'm thirsty."

"I don't think there is anymore water left down there. Just hold out for me a little longer. God will protect us. I'm going to pray for him to take your thirst away."

There she goes again! I couldn't take it anymore, my body was so filled with annoyance and resentment I thought my head would blow. I knew I couldn't say anything. I didn't want to be disrespectful and it was way too hot to start up anyway. I just laid back down. I could hear soft mumbles of prayer coming from her direction. I just closed my eyes and pretended to hear nothing at all. The heat helped me to drift off to sleep for a short nap.

I was snatched from my slumber by the sounds of what seemed to be a house party above us on the next level. People were singing and laughing. The sounds of a second line can be the only thing that could compare. It was like they all had hit a wall and had lost their mind in their stay at the dome. People were leaving their spots near us and going up to see what the commotion was about but our family just sat and listened in hopes that it was for good reasons. People were going up and down, coming back with more than what they left; candy, water, sodas.

A group of Superdome thieves had hit the jackpot some where. A cluster of young men began to come down to show they had items for sell that they knew would turn a profit. They walked down the corridor with loaded pockets screaming out their prices. Hot $5 beers and cigarettes for $2.50 were quickly sold to people hoping to find some kind of escape.

While they did charge for the legal drugs of tobacco and alcohol, they weren't looking to make money off of the water. They were sharing to any person that had their hand out. Some roughly dressed men in their late thirties started down the ramp towards us. They had on dingy wife beaters and jeans that they had to hold up with one hand. In the other they carried things to share with their Superdome neighbors.

"We gonna take care of y'all!" One of the men who was in clear need of some rest yelled out to all of us, "We need to stick together and make sure we live through this. We really gonna take care of y'all." He started to hand out bottles of water to people around us, pulling bottles of water from his sagging pants pockets. Slowly he made his way towards our corner.

My grandma turned her head down to me, "You know those waters are stolen? Mmmhhmmm. You know God wouldn't like this. Don't take the water." She whispered in a demanding demeanor.

"I'm taking that water. I'm thirsty. We all thirsty. Why wouldn't we take it?" I didn't even glance in her direction to avoid missing him walk by.

"Its stolen! What if they put something in it? It could be poisoned." She shook her head and closed the cover of her Bible.

Grandpa Burnell took the first bottle as the man passed. The next was handed to me as well as a silent smile. I gladly gave the stranger a grin back. When he reached my grandmother she smirked sweetly and refused the bottle without any words just a quick shake of her head. The man looked confused. Every other person he compassionately provided a bottle to took it. This was not something he was expecting nor was I.

"Give it to me," my grandpa reached out his hand hoping he would give the water to him for safe keeping, "I'll hold it until she gets some damn sense." The man handed it over to my grandfather while still looking at my grandma as her hands began to thumb through her old Bible again. He soon moved on to other needing souls.

"You can gone ahead and drink that water, Burnell. I don't want it." My grandma stuck her nose in the air and her face looked as if she had just witnessed something repulsive and smelled something vile.

My grandpa took a deep breath in before entertaining her, "Why the hell not, Ludie?"

"You know that water is stolen. Don't pretend you don't know it. You know better than to mess with God's commandments. You better get your life together. You see what He's done here. You need to be worried about going to church and not no stolen water," by the look on her face she felt she had done a good deed by warning God's sheep of what was going to happen if they didn't get their house in order.

"Ludie shut the hell up! You sound like a damn fool, you know that? Maybe God sent the water. Ain't nothing but a damn clown! I don't know why I feed into your dumb ass sometimes!" He threw the water at her feet. "Drink it, don't drink it. You figure it out!"

I grabbed the water before it started to roll away. I tucked it under my leg and opened my journal once more.

"Tyierra, you understand that this isn't right?" she leaned over to me not taking her eyes off of my grandpa.

I gazed over to her, "Neither is dying of thirst. Take this as a blessing and ask for God's grace and mercy later," I pulled the water bottle from underneath my leg and plopped it in her open hand.

Grandma looked into the distance before gripping the water. She slowly opened the bottle and took a drink. To her that was the most unholy water she had ever tasted but it kept her going. Maybe there was a God. Maybe this was our boat and we got on it. Maybe we needed to listen more to the world around us and stop looking for huge miracles to drop at our front door and understand the small ones around us.

# Chapter 14: The Lady in the Purple Pants

*"The trouble when you're doing something illegal is that you know what you're doing. You're lying to your parents, you're lying to your kids. The only person you can't lie to is yourself."*

**-Tommy Chong**

"The shortest distance between two points is a straight line." That's really the only thing that my grandfather ever taught me outside of how to stock shelves where he worked and that all women have a period. He told me this when I got mine for the first time in the sixth grade. That was a bit awkward. I learned mostly social studies and math from school. Long division was the hardest at first. Thank goodness for calculators. There was music class, too. I learned The Jackson Five *Rockin' Robin* and I just could not stop signing it, driving the whole house crazy.

I loved history. We didn't get much of it in elementary but I treasured hearing the past tales from TV. I also liked to hear the stories on a cancelled PBS series called Wishbone. I think most of my affection for literature today comes from that show. The one thing I just could not wrap my head around, and there wasn't much help from the Orleans Parish Public School System, was reading.

"What are you going to be when you grow up, Tyierra?" My grandmother would ask, "A doctor? A lawyer? A model?"

"I want to be a writer!" I would jump in front of my grandparents' TV as they sat listening to my young mind bloom. "I am going to go all over the world and then I am going to write about stuff I see! Then I'ma put it in the newspaper! And magazines!"

I wanted to be a journalist. I had my whole life planned out. I was going to be the face of World News on ABC while also being a writer at Source Magazine in New York City. Those two positions would lead me to my own talk show. When I wasn't filming, I would be writing. I wanted to write books and plays. I wanted to entertain people with the countless story lines drifting around in my head. I just needed some where to put all of my thoughts.

"That's why I need a computer!" I yelled out as I explained my future.

My grandfather would be sitting on the floor with half a bag of shelled raw peanuts waiting to be cracked while the remains of the other half were all over the discolored carpet. He would look up at me, "Girl you know how dumb you sound? You think you gettin' a computer? You got to know how to read which you don't! I wish you get your ass from out in front this TV so I can watch my westerns."

As mean as that may sound, he was right. How could I write if I couldn't read? My grandma would help me by telling me words like "cat" and "red." Being in grade school, I was way past those words. In the fourth grade, is when I first realized seriously I needed to work on reading. My grandmother would take me to the library that is now known as Rosa F. Keller Library and Community Center Uptown on South Broad. I would get books to read that had things to do with faraway places or having pets. The other kids would giggle under their hands as they looked in my direction. I was reading baby books. The books with three to five words on each page and more colorful pictures than anything.

I really do not know how I made it in school. I would try and get people to read chapters ahead of time in front of me if we were supposed to read at home. I'd remember what our homework assignment would be when the teacher would explain it so I didn't have to ask my grandma and my grandpa and they hear how stupid I was. I once tried to remember vocabulary words from the day before that we had to draw pictures of to show our understanding of the word. The teacher was at the board writing the ten words we would work on that night. I memorized them in order. The next day, I brought in my completed assignment and she laughed at me. I had drawn a stick figured man with a muscle that had deflated to reflect the word "weak." However, the word was "week" and had nothing to do with strength. Clearly my confusion was visible. I pretended it was on purpose. It was not.

When I did ask my grandma for help, my grandpa would still be at work or away at the race track. I could remember in the fifth grade having someone write our spelling words on my black desk with her eraser. The only way you could see them during our weekly spelling quiz was if you looked at the perfect angle. Don't get me wrong, I knew some words when I saw them, it was just hard to understand and even harder to spell.

I never gave up my dream of being an author even with my lack of a hefty vocabulary. I tried desperately to persuade my grandfather to get me a laptop. I needed it! I had to have somewhere to put down my stories and plays I wanted to share with the world. Paper was not going to do. I'm not sure what words I was going to use knowing very few, but I had to at least start. Not many people remember the iBooks of yester year but I do. I knew I had to have that tangerine clamshell. As far as I was concerned, all the fancy writers and famous people had those things, so that meant I had to as well.

I continued to beg and beg him for years at every opportunity until he finally broke down at the bus stop on our way home, "Shit girl! Damn I will get you a computer! But you gotta know how to read first!" That is all I wanted. It was all I needed to hear, a little bit of hope and his unintended motivation.

I tried everything I could to get more words in front of me. I would ask classmates what a word was, teachers, and the librarians even if I was a little embarrassed. I put the captions on the TV to see words as people would say them. My favorite was trying to find words that resembled each other like "look" and "book" so to associate one word's sound with the other. Even breaking words apart that had two conjoined words, like lunchbox or backpack, was something I learned from. I was determined to discover the world of reading even if I had to do it on my own. I didn't care how long it would take.

As the years went by, I didn't get a laptop but I did get a few desktop computers. They all were from Rent-A-Center or Aaron's which meant they didn't have that new car smell but they all worked just fine for me. I learned quickly that computers in our house would only be a brief amenity. I was given plenty of really nice things as a child but they were not long after taken away to either pay a bill or feed a habit.

I wasn't the only one he would take from. There were times my grandmother's piece of mind was taken. My grandfather would sit in the bathroom for hours to write her a long six to eight-page letter on how she needed to call the "rent man" and tell him that the few hundred dollars wrapped in the letter he gave her was all they had. Before she would unfold the document, he would already be out the door and on the way to the track. The letter would also say that if she wasn't happy she could leave and to make sure to take all her "shit" with her as if she did she wasn't welcomed back.

When I learned to really understand words, I began to get those same letters myself. In place of the TV he gifted me once was an I.O.U. note. I got another the day he took back a camcorder I asked for the Christmas before. My grandmother got them nearly every first of the month saying something wouldn't be paid.

By the time I got to the sixth grade is when Juney met Dajuan. She hadn't finished high school as she couldn't pass the required tests in the twelfth grade. It was really difficult for her being pregnant with my uncle's baby in her senior year and all. She enlisted the aid of myself to assist her with her homeschool work and take her examinations. All of which my uncle had paid for. Yes, me. The girl who could barely read Charlotte's Web a couple years before was now doing the homework and assessments of a high school senior. I had really learned to be intelligent and if no one else noticed it, my uncle sure did. He made sure I knew how valuable being smart was.

My uncle did try to keep a smile on my face between his father giving me letters. He did not want me forever to be the strange kid in school. He got me a cell phone. It was nothing too fancy; just a little flip phone that I was afraid if I kept flipping it would break. My granddad knew I had it but my uncle ensured him it would be for my safety not for me to talk to boys. He didn't have to worry. Not too many boys were looking in my direction anyway. I still was that ugly duckling. Besides, I was too busy in my head wanting to be a famous writer and was more concerned with people who could get me there.

There weren't too many contacts in my phone outside of my grandparents, uncle, and my Aunt Tressa. The only other names I saved were of those who I knew would help me get to my dream someday. I had a contact set up for Oprah Winfrey, Steven Spielberg, and even Ricki Lake. Why? Because I knew one day, I was going to get the opportunity to meet them. I didn't want to waste their time trying to find a piece of paper to write their number down or lose precious moments creating a new contact in front of them. Strange I know but I have my own way of dreaming.

Another contact I had was Tyler Perry. He was a new name that Dajuan was the first to mention to me, but I fell instantly in love with him. Not in the romantic "*I want to be the mother of your children*" way but in a "*you are giving me real hope*" manner. He was living the dream I wanted. He was black, had such a disconnect from his father that he changed his name, from New Orleans, and was breaking his way into the entertainment world with his words. I knew if he could make it, so could I. I just had to keep pushing.

A short chubby little boy who would wear throwback jerseys to school on dress down days with the tag sticking out the back to show the price ended up stealing my phone from me on the last day of school that year. The next phone I got I did the exact same thing. To this day, I still have some of those wishful thinking contacts in my phone.

On top of the cell, my uncle got me my first pair of name brand shoes. He asked me what I wanted for Christmas and I told him a pair of Allen Iverson's, all black. Juney offered me my first PlayStation but I refused it as I didn't want to come home from school one day and it be gone. I'd rather have a pair of shoes to wear. Nothing too fancy just something above thrift store and Walmart.

I did finally get that laptop. I guess my grandfather saw some potential in me. It was the same process, however, rented from a furniture store and it was no tangerine clamshell iBook. It was a used Dell laptop that had huge scratches on the corner but it was mine and I didn't care. My grandfather had really come through on this one. He told me no matter what, that laptop was mine and it wasn't going anywhere. I was officially a writer.

That same year as a seventh grader I beat out several eight graders in an essay contest and I still have the certificate from winning to prove it. When they announced the top three of the seventh graders and I was not among them, I was a bit disappointed but then hearing my name alongside those who were one grade above me made me feel like I was on my way. It was only a middle school competition but it was me who had won! All thanks to that laptop and the spell check features. I can still remember some of the stories I had started to write. I knew that they weren't perfect. I knew I had a long way to go to being the next Tyler Perry but I sure was going to keep trying.

One of the novels I had started and will never forget was about a fifteen-year-old girl who everyone called Cupcake from the blocks of Atlanta. Cupcake had a four-month-old daughter who she couldn't provide for as she was damn near a baby herself. She turned to stealing as an option. The first chapter started off in the middle of a normal day for her:

Those little Korean people are gonna reach under that register one day, pull out that 9mm, and pop me right in the back of my head. But I had to hit that little side store up. Its' not like I took any money. I just grabbed a fist full of diapers for my baby girl waiting at home. These won't even last me two days. I needed to move fast. One because baby girl is waiting alone and two I think the little Asian lady saw me rip open the package. If she knows any better she will just let this happen. She don't know what else I got in this bag. It may be something to change the life of her family and end hers.

The story would go on about her mother who always had a needle in her arm and her father who was shot and killed when she was six. She would bloom after more tragedy would occur in her little world but it would not be in the positive direction. That was going to be my first novel. I would doodle in a notebook on my way home from school small ideas I wanted to put in the book I was to complete and share it with the world. So many ideas of her becoming the leader of a drug operation after being forced to kill her own mother. But then one day it was gone.

My grandpa was walking next to me down the Parkway when I found out "Don't be scared, Tyierra," he said as he limped down the road, "Someone came in the house today but I don't think they will be back." At that moment the street was quiet. No cars were passing and not a single soul was to be seen. It was just the two of us.

"Someone broke into the house? Did they take anything? How did this happen?" I was scared. *What if they were still in there? What if they would come back?* I found myself clung to the side of my grandfather's body nearly in tears from fear.

"Naw, I let them in," I pulled away confused as he looked straight forward while speaking, "It was a lady I knew from the store. I'd seen her a couple times. She wanted some water, something to drink. I went in the kitchen to get her a RC cola and all I heard was her flying out of the house then saw her takeoff sprinting down the street."

He continued to tell me she had stolen items from the house. While there was a list of things the one that popped out, the only one I could think about, was my laptop. She had stolen my laptop. All of my stories, my plays, my hard work, was gone!

"Did you find her?" I asked as I felt my face become hot and my fist clench, "We have to find her! What's her name? She has my laptop!"

Of course he couldn't give me a name because he didn't know one. All I could think about was the millions of times he and my grandmother had told me not to talk to strangers and there he was letting one in the house. He did remember what she was wearing. He told me she had on a mustered color shirt and purple pants. He described her as having nappy dark brown hair and an old pair of white tennis shoes, much like the pair he was wearing. He explained she may have been homeless.

"Why did you let her in the house?" I was not only filled with curiosity but anger. I really wanted to know what would influence him to let a homeless dirty shoe wearing woman in the house and I was barely allowed to play with classmates across the street.

"She said she was thirsty," He glanced over to me to see if I was listening to him. That I was.

With an itchy throat and moist eyes I replied, "The lady in the purple pants has all my stories and stuff. I wanted it back!"

"Write new ones! You must have something on that computer you not supposed to since you want it back so bad! You act like she stole your words!"

But she had stolen my words. This lady in purple pants had stolen all of me. He would never understand what it had done and how I felt knowing my hard work was gone. I don't think he would even care. While he had lost interest in me getting the laptop back, he did make sure he let me know that he filed a police report to avoid having to continue to pay the weekly bill to the rent-to-own company.

For a few weeks, I felt like a detective. I searched the house for clues. *Maybe her strands of hair fell off. Maybe she left finger prints on the door.* That's what watching Forensic Files will do to you. It wasn't just at home. Every woman on the street was a suspect now. I did my own personal line up every time I was on the bus or went into my grandpa's job. It did no good. My laptop and my hard work was gone.

I gave up on my dream. I put the keyboard, or in my case the pencil, down. Not because everything I had been working on was probably erased, but because maybe this was a sign from God. I needed to stop writing as it was no good. I just finally learned words that were made up of more than four letters. What was I thinking? I was going to be just like everyone else; old weave, long nails, two gold teeth, and three kids. Just like my grandfather had imaged for me and just like it was intended for me to be. I needed to get used to it.

I started to hang with Dajuan a lot more. She truly epitomized the negative essence of New Orleans. If I was going to be a true citizen of the birthplace of Jazz, she

193

would be the one to teach me. She introduced me to fake contacts that she bought me from the hair salon. They were gray and made my eyes itch. That fad didn't last long as my uncle told me to stop covering up my already pretty hazel eyes. She also tried to pierce a second hole in my ears with a home kit. She got one ear done and I told her no more. It was way too painful. For a couple days, I was walking around with one earring in my ear and I could swear everyone was looking at how stupid I was.

She also introduced me to beer. She gave me a sip of her Heineken and it was the nastiest flavor I had ever had the displeasure of letting drop on my tongue. The green bottled beer tasted like dirty water. I still cannot drink one of those things till this day. I did get a sip of her strawberry daiquiri a couple months later from Fat Tuesday and that wasn't half bad. She was the only friend I had at the time. Or maybe I was hers.

Then one day, while walking to Cajun's Seafood she asked me, "You know Mr. Burnell pawned that laptop, right?"

"No, somebody stole it from the house," I responded attempting to defend him. I knew he wouldn't do that to me after swearing to me he wouldn't take it back, "He didn't pawn it."

"Purple pants, Tyierra? Please," She took a deep breath, "Yo' uncle had to beg them people not to haul his stupid self off to jail. He got the laptop out of the pawn store and brought it back to the store. You better be glad he know people or he would have been locked up. Don't tell your uncle, he told me not to tell you but his daddy stupid as hell."

Could this be true? I was told by my uncle that he had gotten in trouble for the same situation before I was old enough to remember and spent a weekend in a jail cell so I knew he was capable. But why?

Every moment before that day I trusted my grandfather. Through every bad situation, every rentless night, all of the hungry days, and the moments of being called dumb I trusted him because he told me the truth of how messed up our position was or how stupid I looked. Even with the long letters explaining to me why the birthday money I got from Juney was needed for the light bill I had faith in him. But if lying to me about a mysterious woman in dirty shoes wasn't enough he just didn't care that my dream had vanished.

I did pick up my notebook and pen again after that. I had to talk to someone on how I felt and my pen was the only thing that understood. I didn't bring it up again to neither my grandfather nor his son. It was pointless. If it was true I would hate him even more and if it wasn't I would still always have my doubts. My faith in my grandfather went out the door with the lady in the purple pants.

# Chapter 15: "Don't Lose It Now! I Need You!"

*One person's craziness is another person's reality."*
**-Tim Burton**

Friday was here but it felt like we were stuck in a loop of Monday; like nothing more had been done. If anything, it had gotten worst. It was reported a bit of relief had arrived as National Guard troops drove some food and water into the city but I hadn't seen much of it. The walls were covered with aggravation and the air was thick with a terrible odor. Those who were stuck at the Louis Armstrong New Orleans International Airport days of living in fear was over. The over twenty thousand people shut in there would find freedom by way of one of fifteen airlines who were told they were allowed to transport them to other safe locations.

Those trying to enter Gretna, LA were not so lucky. It was said that local authorities of Jefferson Parish was stopping entrance to the safe place by blocking the roads and firing shots in the air over the heads of those trying to escape. This was a decision made by Police Chief Arthur Lawson who still has no regrets of his decision. Even though that choice led to turning away families at the Crescent City Connection with small children all because he wanted to prevent looting in his town.

This was only days before national news starting covering what was going on at the New Orleans Greyhound Bus Terminal, minutes away from the dome. Burl Cain the former warden at Angola's State Penitentiary, a maximum-security prison farm, oversaw what was referred to as Camp Greyhound. There was no use in taking the criminals to Orleans Parish Prison as they would normally do. There was no power, no food, and nearly 6,800 inmates who were trapped in their cells. Some inmates shared being stuck in their boxes with water up to their waist. Others were forced to eat tissue and toothpaste for a lack of options.

Guards had left the prison leaving its guests locked in their cells, which made the inmates curious about what would happen to them next. Later it was discovered that the guards refused to go back inside the prison to save the others for the lack of visibility. Those who did manage to escape were met right outside the doors by officers in boats who hauled them off to places like the Broad Street overpass. There they waited in the heat for days without water or blockage from the sun.

But the flooded cells did not stop the lockups. Over 220 looters, men and women, that were caught on the streets stealing were brought to the temporary jail at Camp Greyhound. They were then photographed, fingerprinted, and thrown into chain-link cages.

No official word was passed to my family and I that buses were being loaded to take us away from our nightmare but outside those walls it was finally happening. Texas was kind enough to open two more large facilities. With the crowd being so enormous outside, my grandfather decided that staying in the dome was our best option. Taking our chances outside would leave us exposed to the New Orleans summer sun. It was just better to stay in and continue waiting. This was without knowing that buses were being loaded to get people to liberty only mere yards from where we laid.

The heat still danced around on the inside of the dome as people rested. I caught my grandmother looking at me every now and again, deep in thought about what had transpired in the last few days. I sat thinking about how much the world probably had changed on the streets of the Crescent City. My life would never be the same. Everything I knew was over. Every memory I had was washed away literally and figuratively.

Even the memories I had not made yet would probably never happen within the city limits.

*I don't have my license yet. I don't even know how to drive.*

*What about senior year at McMain?*

*Prom? As if they will let me go to prom but still.*

It was the first time I had stepped inside of the Superdome in my fifteen years. I wanted to see a Saints game in the stands and cheer with my black and gold attire on just like all the other enthusiasts but in that moment I knew it would never happen.

*Would I see another Mardi Gras?*

*No more King Cakes?*

*No more bounce music or second lines?*

*No more hot Cheetos, pickles, or frozen cups?*

All of the culture I knew was gone and it wasn't coming back. Though I was surrounded by hundreds of people, I never felt more alone than in that thought.

In the middle of my contemplations, I heard a shouting voice from down the hall. A woman appeared with streams of tears falling from her face. Her shirt didn't fit her properly, exposing one of her shoulders and it was clear signs of the lack of a proper bath. Her pants were red and visibly a few sizes too small while her hair was wild and disordered. What was the most distracting was not her hair but her words.

"The city is on fire! This city is on fire!" Hearts dropped as eyes turned to see the mysterious woman and then turned back to each other. She screamed at everyone who stared in her direction, "Why are y'all just sittin' there? Don't you hear me? The city is on fire! We are in hell!"

When she screamed her voice cracked as she tried to warn us all. No one moved. Her defeat got the best of her as she began to tug on her already stretched shirt; dragging it below her knees.

"All y'all gonna die in here! The dome in on fire! New Orleans is on fire!" After throwing her hands open and in the air signaling she was giving up on our section, she slowly moved out of sight carrying tears on her cheeks while still spreading her message. My grandmother grabbed my hand and squeezed to let me know things will be okay and so that I could feel connected to another human being. I squeezed back.

"Crack head," my grandfather shook his head in disbelief, "We are surrounded by crack heads, Uncle Toms, and looney toons."

It was not clear if the demented woman was referring to explosions that had occurred at a local chemical storage plant in New Orleans that caused the break out of fires that day or if she was just not all there upstairs. I didn't want to think she was crazy or even a bit influenced by narcotics but I had to study the other options. It was scary to consider that God had sent us all to hell or that we were living in it. Still in our fear, no one moved. We just continued to do the nothing we were doing before she appeared. All but one.

His screams were not understood at first but it was easy to see he was not happy to be trapped as he walked closer. Everyone carried worry on their face as they witnessed yet another emotional outbreak. The middle aged man wearing a soiled t-shirt and discolored ball cap was yelling with frustration at the site that had just passed. His skin was dark and dried much like the jeans he wore. His face was covered with salt and pepper colored stubbles from lack of shaving and his hands showed signs of years of hard labor.

"This ain't right! We got babies and women in here! Crack heads running around screaming! I'ma figure this shit out myself!" As he stormed by, he roared words of determination to discover what had us stuck. "They can put a million words on a microchip the size of a penny, but you mean to tell me they can't get my ass out of this Superdome?" his words were simple but true. I never got to see him come back passed us. Maybe he found his way out. Something he deserved; we all deserved. But time didn't seem to be on our side.

Soon after 9/11 in New York there was a national response to help the city, our country, find justice and mourn. All across the US, people flew fags, wore pins and t-shirts while as many hands as possible helped rebuild New York. This country stood strong. I do not down play 9/11's devastation on this country. It truly was a senseless act of terror and I commend the government's quick response and the country's dedication to wiping away the tears of their fellow Americans. There is no strength like that of New York City. Yet, during those moments on the floor of the Superdome, as a US citizen, I couldn't even use the restroom without feelings of disgust.

I can't help but feel pushed to the side when I think of how the government responded to the December 26, 2004 Indian Ocean earthquake and tsunami. Our humanitarian response to assist the west coast of Sumatra, Indonesia led to us pledging $35 Million. Two days, just two days, after the tsunami, a time when most of everyone was on holiday break, they managed to scrape together millions of dollars to donate to a country on the other side of the world. Yet, during those moments on the floor of the Superdome, as a US citizen, I couldn't even get a bottle of water.

Everyone went back to waiting as things calmed again. I looked down to my long nails that had cakes of dirt under them. I soon felt the need for something to eat as my belly rumbled, a scream for food. Though it was the first few days of the month, I knew my grandfather didn't have access to any of his social security checks being that we all were trapped. Swaying around in the back of my head was how we were going to live, eat, anything without access to money. Then I realized I may not get out of there at all to be worried about money. I bounced my head off the wall behind me and adjusted my sites to the ceiling. Sweat ran down my neck and I could feel the eczema rash under my nose becoming irritated, matching the rashes in the creases of my arms. As I brutally rubbed away my itch, my thoughts decided to run away from me.

*Terrian is dead.*

*Drika is dead.*

*Juney is dead.*

*They are doing this to us on purpose, to keep us here. There are no buses.*

*We are going to die here. Oh my God, we are going to die. I'm not ready to die!*

My fears hit me all at once. Racing thoughts of being trapped behind the doors of the dome filled me. My heart began to beat faster thinking of my uncle's lifeless body floating down Tchoupitoulas Street. I thought of me dying and all of the life I hadn't seen yet. The walls seemed to be closing in on me. The air was heavier than I remembered. My hands began to tremble. I had never felt this way before.

I looked over to my grandfather who was occupying his time by reading bits of scrap paper that was left from cleaning out his wallet. Deep quick breaths in and out caught his attention.

"Girl, what in the hell is wrong with you?" he yelled as he looked up from the receipts he was hording. I could tell he was fed up with new situations arising so suddenly.

"I don't know," I managed to drag the words from my mouth, "I can't breathe," Having asthma and not always having access to the proper medicine, I learned to control my breathing but this was no asthma spell. I was having a panic attack.

"Burnell!" my grandmother grabbed my hand again, "Do something she can't breathe!"

"Ludie, calm down. Come on, Tyierra. Let's go get some air. Just calm down and get up," I followed my grandfather's directions and stood up gradually to slow the feeling of fainting. We began to walk out towards the opening of the dome.

As we moved closer to the exit, I could feel myself coming back to a normal state of mind. The negative thoughts were leaving but would soon be replaced with the images of those around me. The walk was filled with the smell of filth. People were irritated, confused, and depressed all in the same tick. Trash stuck to the floors because of the liquid it swam in. The joy in children that was once there was gone. They sat with their backs to the wall lifeless, no color in them anymore. It felt as if we were all on an infomercial asking for donations. This was not how life was supposed to be lived.

My grandpa and I walked outside of the glass doors of the dome to the concourse around the arena that gave clear view to the 50-yard bridge that connected it to the New Orleans Centre which had flooded due to the storm. The heat immediately took our breaths away as we walked into the crowd. People were everywhere waddling in an ocean of trash. The debris in some places was nearly waist high, just as the water was in the city. Moving pass other's confined to the dome I could see old suitcases people left behind, dirty diapers, and even children's toys.

A tampon applicator rolled as I kicked it accidentally with my foot while proceeding to a clearing in the crowd but the odor did not lessen. The smell was worst than I experienced inside due to the heat pounding on the wasteland day in and out. It was obvious people had started to release their bodily fluids outside instead of punishing themselves by using what was once known as a restroom indoors.

I began to choke on the thick air. My grandfather, who was following close behind, patted me on my back. I turned to him.

"I don't know about this one, girlie," he called me by one of the nicknames he used often, "We in deep doo doo this time."

His words made me chuckle a bit. I looked down to the ground and moved my foot around the trash that was left behind, "What are we going to do?"

"Wait. That's all we can do. Wait and pray that everything goes our..." before my granddad could finish his words he was stopped by a woman's screams.

"HE HAS A HOOK! HE HAS A HOOK! RUN!" an unknown females voice yelled from a crowd of people. I looked up to see about a dozen set of eyes staring at me. It didn't take long for me to realize it was not me they were gazing at but instead the man with the large hay hook behind me.

He wore a tan colored bucket hat and his skin was dark, much darker than my own. His shorts matched his head covering and his shirt was once white. He was surrounded by a small circle of trash as if he was creating a circle of protection, something that was spoken about in the movie Skeleton Key released only a couple weeks before. I guess he didn't learn that that circle of protection would only keep him from leaving it. Hook

Man clutched the wooden handle firmly as he swung his weapon violently. His eyes were slammed shut as he oscillated with no intended victim, screaming only two words over and over, "GET BACK!"

I fell backwards trying to avoid being his first fatality landing on my hands and bottom. My grandfather was there to pick me up out of the filth on the ground. My fear forced me to grab him and hug tight. He dragged my away from Hook Man's rage. He tried to pull me off of him but he could not get me to release. I was too afraid to let go but what was worst, I didn't want my Grandpa Burnell to see me cry.

He hadn't really seen me cry since I was in diapers. It didn't feel right to show my pain to him or my grandmother. I never really got a whooping or even so much as a spanking for bad behavior because there was little room for me to cut up. Pain from me they witness but it was one thing to be in the hospital for asthma and pneumonia not being able to breathe type of pain and another for me to have this emotional break down. All of what had happen, I did not show weakness by crying in front of him.

The thought of spending another moment in the Superdome started to hurt me so bad, I couldn't hold it in anymore. My mind would not let me keep going. I felt the tears streaming down my cheek. I started to make sobbing sounds and tried to pull him closer to me.

"Are you crying?" my grandfather was as surprised as I was.

"No," I replied trying to avoid the conversation all together.

"Yes you are crying! Look at me!" He finally was strong enough to pull me away from his safety and held me by my upper arm, "Snap out of it, Tyierra!"

His words only made the tears pour faster, "I can't! I can't be here anymore!" I knew others could hear me sobbing out but I couldn't see them as my vision was blurred from the weeping. My mind was not stable. I was not stable. I just kept thinking I wanted to go home. Then more tears would fall from my eyes because I knew there was no home to go back to. My family was falling apart and my memories were floating into the Gulf of Mexico. I could no longer take it. Katrina had defeated me.

"You gonna let this beat you? I can't believe I have to say this to you! You can't let this beat you! It's a little water and a little wind! Ludie needs you in there! I need you! *You can't loose it now!*"

# Chapter 16: You Can't Have a Rainbow without the Rain

*"It sounds so simple, but if you just be yourself, you're different than anyone else"*

**-Tony Bennett**

### *Strong*

*No female can touch me*
*No male can doubt me*
*Cuz I am who I am*
*"Are you mixed?" They ask*
*"You too cute, you gotta be mixed"*
*As if we don't all come in different shapes and shades*
*Naw, I'm not mixed*
*But I do have the waist of a woman*
*And the mind of man*
*Anything you're capable of, I am too*
*And I bet you $100 I can do it better than you*
*Been through it all*
*The good and the bad*
*So you can't scare me, I fear nothing*
*Not lions, tigers, or bears*
*I had to fight to get everything I have, so it's mine*
*I'll never look for their handouts*
*Not from a stranger or a friend*
*Because loyalty? Trust? Respect?*
*Those things don't... hashtag trend*
*So let me get up and do this for me*
*Let me use my words to cut these chains free*

I'm just going to keep chanting my song
And when I loose my words don't think that I'm wrong
Go ahead and ask me all the questions you want
So I can tell you not one lie
Make sure you offer me the same truths
Because you won't be able to pull the wool over my eyes
See, I've seen it all and done it twice
Lived in houses with candles for lights
Had nothing to eat but uncooked rice
But now?
I feed myself with more than just rations
But the passion
To keep smashin'
Through whatever happens
Are these Payless or Red Bottom
I mean really Who gives a damn
For them it's prolly cheaper to match their shoes to their
purse
Than It is to match their actions to their words
But that's not me
I'm not just some average black girl in boots
Playing GI Joe
Naw, I'm your worst nightmare who learned her worth
Something you should have never let me know
I've seen every kind of hate, known all sorts of wrong
But every silent battle on my character

Has only made me strong


Music has always been my escape. No matter if it
was the soulful hums of The Temptations, Aretha Franklin,
and Chaka Khan, the mix of music during my favorite era

of the 90s like NWA, Keith Sweat, and R. Kelly or the more recent musical icons of today like The Weekend, Bruno Mars, Drake, and Cardi B. Sounds of music is like a warm hug to me. My favorite song? Juvenile Back that Thang Up. I just can't help myself when "taking over for the 99 and the 2000" flow through my earbuds.

It can take you to memories you didn't even know you had stored in the back of your head. Some songs can make me smile, a few will bring back memories that make me want to cry, and then there are the songs out there that can make me really want to fight someone. Music we hear on the radio are the pages to someone's life; they are poems from someone's diary sung to a beat. As I listen I would close my eyes and imagine being in their world and getting a firsthand experience.

It was early one morning when I was still lying on the sofa waiting for my grandfather to come out of the bathroom. I was listening to the lyrics of TLC songs that I had on a scratched bootleg CD. My eyes were closed as I moved my hands and arms to resemble their Waterfalls music video. I can still hear the words banging in my ear:

*Little precious has a natural obsession for temptation*
*But he just can't see*
*She give him loving that his body can't handle*
*But all he can say is, "Baby, it's good to me"*
*One day he goes and takes a glimpse in the mirror*
*But he doesn't recognize his own face*
*His health is fading and he doesn't know why*

*Three letters took him to his final resting place*
*Y'all don't hear me*

"Tyierra!" my grandfather yelled my name as I was imagining dancing on water in baggy pants right next to T-Boz, Chilli and the late Left Eye.

I jumped and pulled the foam earphones off my head, "Yes?"

"You acting like you can't hear me? Take that shit off your head and get ready to go to school!" I slowly pulled the headphones and the CD player that my uncle had gotten me from my close grip. I put them under the raised sofa while my grandfather wasn't looking. I just wanted to be able to find it when I got back home that afternoon. I grabbed my bag, my keys, and a couple slices of gum from a pack next to my grandpa's wallet and headed to the bus stop where Drika would be waiting.

My grandfather allowed me to ride the public bus on my own while attending McMain. It was mostly because my grandma was in California at the time. If she would have known this was going on, she would be on the first thing moving back towards New Orleans. She had been out there for a while but I can tell each time we spoke on the phone that she missed her family. I figured she just wanted to continue the distance between herself and my grandfather. I still do not fully understand why she would purposely return to New Orleans. Maybe it was for my grandpa. Maybe it was for her son. Maybe it was for me.

On the days Drika wasn't there at the bus stop with me, I would just sit there and watch as the RTA would pass me by. As long as I wasn't going to be late to school, why not take a few moments of silence. If not that, I'd take a different bus route that was longer just to get off the corner in case my grandfather decided to pop up.

I sometime would close my eyes and listened to the traffic passing. The sound would remind me of the ocean crashing against the shore. The roar of the bus as my eyes were shut riding my way to my first class would be the base of a song I would create in my mind. To that song I'd then create a music video full of dancing and color. Then I would open my eyes and see I am still in the same place I was before.

That day I went straight to school. It was going to be a busy morning and I wanted to get to homeroom early. School was something I did finally start to enjoy. I had began to adjust to those around me and grew into myself as the years passed. The negative people did not bother me as they once did. More than anything, it was my time to get away from who I was and be a normal girl.

It was clearly seen that I was excited to go to school and it was painful knowing I was going home at the end of the day. Facial expressions would give me away. My grandfather knew school was my bliss and it was more like play time with tests than an actual educational institute. When I would cause trouble, or what he considered as trouble, that is what he would take from me in place of giving me a whooping. He would take school. The day after he was displeased with my behavior, he would force me to stay home or go to work with him and help put stock on the shelves. I suppose it was because there wasn't much of anything else he could take.

It was not until I was in the middle of one of my wild day dreams of being a music video director on my way home from school that I realized what I had done. I patted my pants pockets, went through my backpack two, three, four times. I even looked in the area around me in my double seat on the South Claiborne bus as they may have fallen out of my pocket when I sat down. I had left my keys in my locker right next to my PE uniform. I just took in a deep breath to think everything out.

I caught one more bus to get closer to the end of the Louisiana Avenue Parkway that we lived on. Once getting off, I started my walk towards the house, hiking right by where my grandfather worked. I refused to go to the store and ask him for his set of keys.

*He is going to be pissed. He gone think I lost them and somebody is going to break in the house or something. Then he gone say I can't ride the bus alone no more. I'm just not going to go over there.*

I knew that my 17-year-old neighbor Riana would let me use her house phone to call my uncle. He had a spare key and I'm sure would let me in the house to avoid alerting my grandfather. I wouldn't need my key again until the next afternoon as my grandpa would lock up the following morning.

I walked up to the front steps of Riana's house and knocked. She opened the squeaky door and looked down to me with a smile covering her flawless face. The tall and thin, dark brown skinned teen popped her hip to the side as she flaunted a pair of capri jeans and a wife beater decorated with pint and blue fabric paint that she had created herself. She didn't have on any socks or shoes so I could see her smooth skin starting from her toes all the way to the cuff of her pants.

She had a single tattoo of the nickname her older and ignorant boyfriend had given her. I believe it was Honey but I really tried to avoid looking for it. I can't even recall if it was on her back or her arm. I tried my best to not think about that male caller of hers. It was all out of jealousy. I just couldn't decide if I was bitter she had a boyfriend and I couldn't or if it was that she had a boyfriend and I couldn't have her.

Riana was not my first crush on the ladies and it would definitely not be my last. For years, I fought my obsession with women because of how many people seen it as the strange road to travel. I already had enough unusual specifics about myself going on in life. Trying to explain to the world that I was also in love with the grace of women was out of the question.

But I was. I've secretly preferred the presence of a woman verses that of a man since the second grade when I fell in love with Ms. London, a teacher at A.H Wilson who had hazel eyes. For one they smell better. That right there is enough. They also are sweet, honest and more trustworthy. Not to leave out they give life to this world. Women are emotional beings and when they fall in love it is just that...love; it is not about adding another notch to their belts. Not to mention they are so soft and nice to stare at.

While I did have crushes on women all throughout grade and high school, I didn't have my real first experience until I turned twenty for fear of judgement. There was this one girl, Christina, who I thought I could really see myself growing old with. I later found out that she was never actually interested in girls as she danced off into the sunset with an ex-boyfriend. It was just some experiment to her. While it wounded me, I convinced myself that maybe it was best. Perhaps it really wasn't right to have those emotions towards women and I should stop thinking about them in that manner. I should instead enjoy the experience and move on. I never really learned to let go of that feeling of being with a woman but I needed to learn myself.

That feeling of me wishing to be with a woman was something I couldn't shake when Riana was around, however. And there she was again. Standing in her threshold. Waiting for me to speak.

"Can I use your phone? I'm locked out of the house," I tugged on the adjustable straps of my bag to avoid eye contact for fear of blushing.

"Yea. Hold on," She went back inside to grab her wireless house phone for my use. As she handed it to me, she threw me another grin before sitting her body on the steps to get some air and wait for me to complete my call.

I began to dial my uncle. The first couple of rings went to voicemail. I figured he didn't want to answer a number he was not familiar with. He finally answered after half a dozen tries.

"Hello?" I could hear the radio dispatch in the background letting me know he was driving around his King Cab.

"Juney," I gripped the phone tightly hoping he was nearby, "Can you come open the door? I left my keys at school."

"Where you at? Go to the store and get pop key!" he replied.

"Listen, Juney, he's gone be mad I don't have my key. I'm right here by the house. Can you just please open the door?"

My uncle took in a deep breath and responded, "Yeah, I'm on the way just stay there. Who phone is this?"

"The girl next door," I looked towards Riana. She waved to shoot a silent hello.

"Alright, just stay there," He hung up.

I handed the phone back to my neighbor and took a seat next to her.

"Thank you," I offered her my appreciations.

She looked at me and responded with, "Your welcome. You need to do something with this hair." She rubbed a few flyaway strains back in place on my head. My hair was pulled back into a low braid exposing my large forehead. She was a pro at doing hair and had even put a drawstring ponytail in for me once. My enormous forehead was still visible but at least my hair was neat. We got the sandy red and blond pony from the hair store one street over on Washington.

Riana's hair was never a mess, I wished she would teach me how to look like her. Being a 14-year-old girl with a very small exposure to combing hair and fashion, I sometimes felt like a little boy. I never wore the same clothes as the other girls in my class, or the shoes. My hair was never cute for long. I tried to put ponytails in my hair on my own before and it was a disaster. The ponytail would be long and silky and then there was my nappy blondish hair that didn't match the extensions to begin with.

I tried to wear a donut shaped bun using extensions my uncle's ex-wife left around that were nearly jet black. When I got to school, everyone asked me if I burnt my donut. It was not appealing.

"Yeah, I know. I just don't know what to do with it. I'm going to dye it or something," I shrugged my shoulders.

"You stupid if you dye your hair!" Riana pulled back surprised I would say anything about coloring my mane, "You know how many bald head women out here running around mixing hair dyes together right now to get this color? You better not do nothing with no color! You would be so cute with some curly micros though." She ran her hands over my hair once more. Her touch made me close my eyes and filled me with a sense of security. It only lasted for a split second but it felt like much longer. Then her phone rang.

"Hello? Boy, where you at? Yea she right here, hold on," she handed the phone back to me.

"Hey, you close yet?" I asked assuming it was my uncle.

He took in yet another deep breath, "Pop wants you to go to the store."

"What?" My head dropped. "Why did you tell him? I can't believe you, Juney! Why couldn't you..."

"Tee I'm working! Just go over there and get the dang key! He ain't even mad!" he disconnected the call.

I handed the phone over to Riana and picked myself up to head towards the store. I'm sure she could see the disappointment in my face. I said my good-byes. As I walked down the block I could hear Riana close her door. I passed some kids I knew just coming home from school going in the opposite direction. I didn't engage with them as I was deep in thought to how I was going to tell my grandpa that the keys weren't lost. I knew exactly where they were. I just forgot them in my locker.

I crossed the main street and found myself in the parking lot of Aeren's Supermarket at the corner of Washington and South Dorgenois. I had my story down pack and I knew he was going to believe me. It wasn't like I was lying. I knew exactly where they were.

At the entrance to the store I saw one of my grandfather's co-workers, Gerald. He was a dark skinned man, around six foot two, who was losing his hair. Being deaf, everyone called him No Speak. He worked in the meat department in the back to avoid interacting with the customers. As I got closer to him, his bubbly personality waved radically in my direction. I waved back while grinning and in our own way asked how the day was going. He had just finished his shift and was about to head home. He was able to read my lips and verified that what I assumed he was saying was true. I ended our visual conversation and continued towards the entrance of the store.

Before I could place my hand on the door, the automatic feature opened it for me. And there he stood. My grandfather was there waiting on me. He came rushing out of the door like a lion after a gazelle. I was stuck in the headlights of the situation and did not move.

218

His right hand raised to the sky and came down on my face with a full force of his being. I instantly could feel the blood rushing to my cheek. The deaf butcher had witnessed my punishment. His usually cheery face had vanished. I was ashamed. All because of some keys.

"You must think I'm a damn fool!" My grandfather screamed at me. "I know what you been doing! It's nothing to do with no keys! I know where you were!"

*Oh no, he knows about Riana.*

*How? How does he know? What does he think he knows?*

*What is he going to do to me? What is he going to say?*

"You running around here just like your dumb ass mamma! What little boy house did you call from? I hope he got room because you keep it up that's where you going to be!" He pointed in the direction of an imaginary lover I had. He wasn't concerned with Riana. He thought it was some boy again. And with no surprise, it was because of the past history of my mother.

I truly believe my real mother Yolanda was the reason behind his signs of PTSD. Any symptom of her in me, any kind of flashback of that woman, would trigger my grandfather to flip out. He even questioned my period being late time after time while in high school. If he didn't see enough menstrual pad wrappers in the trashcan, I must be pregnant.

The diary I kept he finally got a hold to. One day, while laying in bed writing and keeping to myself I seemed to telepathically enraged my grandfather. He

219

felt I was keeping secrets from him but sharing them with the pages of a red and white journal I kept under my mattress while I slept. He stormed in the room and snatched it from my grip. I begged him not to read it but my words went unprocessed. Instead, he sat in the bathroom for hours and read every last word. It was nothing too bad but it was enough for him to be pissed at my existence. I never put anything in there about feelings for girls but I did write about other crushes I had on people at school using their initials. I also wrote just how much I hated being apart of that family. Nothing was for myself anymore after that.

I decided to do something different. I knew I couldn't put the pen down and stop myself from wanting to express who I was using words. I then turned my journal entries into poetry, much like my favorite singing artists who expressed themselves in their lyrics. This way only I would know what I really meant and who I was referencing.

It was moments like the slap that I knew I didn't have time to cry. He never allowed me to explain what really happened. I was forever labeled. I didn't get my keys until a few days later. As normal, I had to stay home from school to avoid hooking up with some fictional man. I really hated my grandfather. I'm sure it was out of protection in his own way but there is a thin line between safeguarding your child and suffocating them.

I never disrespected my grandfather no matter how much of a pain he was, but I always wondered who my real father was and if I was at all like him. I wondered if he would accept me for who I was; big forehead, women loving, light skinned, and all. My biological mother never told me much, my grandfather didn't talk about him at all, and my grandmother would only say he was a nice man who worked at the airport in LA. I hoped he was the American musician Charlie Wilson but it was a stretch. My father's name on the birth certificate I had was Charles Curtis Wilson. When I became an adult I wanted to find out more about who I was by finding the other half of me. I wanted to find my real father.

I was twenty-six when I discovered myself Googling private investigators. I found one that wasn't too expensive and handed over a few hundred dollars with hopes in finding him. I gave them the only information I had on the mystery of my life: his name was Charles Curtis Wilson, he was born August 13th and his last known job was the LAX in Los Angeles. I didn't think it would be enough, but it was. Within a week, I had a phone number of the man who could be my real father sent to me via email.

It took a couple days before I called. The nervousness in me slowed my fingers from dialing. I rang the number and at first hung up before I got an answer. I was afraid. *What if he never wanted me? What if he denies even knowing Yolanda was carrying me? What if Yolanda lied and this isn't the right man at all? What if he doesn't like that I have a college degree or how tall I am? What if he doesn't like that I like girls?* I couldn't take anymore rejection. I was going to rip up the sticky I had written his number on and walk away from the possible dismissal all together.

I didn't have time to think anymore as the number called me back. I decided to answer.

"Hello?" I braced myself for disappointment.

"Did someone just call this number?" the voice sounded so familiar yet I had never heard it before.

"Yes. Is this Charles Wilson?" I asked.

"Yeah this is he."

"Do you remember someone named Yolanda?"

The phone went silent. Those five seconds of quiet were the longest of my life. The voice cleared his throat before speaking again, "Is this Tyierra?"

I couldn't believe it. He knew my name and he knew I existed. A chill came over me. I could feel the indicators of crying starting to overtake me as I answered, "Yes. This is Tyierra Wilson." I decided to throw in my last name to maybe help him understand why I was calling after all these years.

It was as if I could hear his smile through the phone. "Tyierra, I've been looking for you."

# Chapter 17: Put the Weapons Down

*"For to be free is not merely to cast off one's chains, but to live in a way that respects and enhances the freedom of others."*

**-Nelson Mandela**

I could see the emotions in my grandfather's eyes as we could still hear the thunder of the crowd shocked by Hook Man. It was as if he wanted to be nice to me or if he wanted to show he really cared but couldn't because he didn't know how. Sitting right next to the emotional love in his eyes for me was fear. He was just as afraid as I was but being the man of the family he felt he couldn't show any weakness.

"You can't lose your mind right now. Too much depends on you keeping a straight head! Just please. I need you and I don't need too often," His grip slowly lightened and his hands fell to his side. I wiped the little bit of wetness away from my cheeks and hoped that my red eyes and runny nose would not be noticed. We started our walk up again, this time in the direction opposite of the commotion. We paced in silence. My mind was filled with sensations of being apart of something greater than myself. I did have to be strong. I had been through a lot and I was not going to let something like this break me.

I walked as he limped a little through all of the garbage surrounding the arena, zigzagging through the gathering of the New Orleans citizens. I caught Grandpa Burnell glancing over to me a few times to identify what state of mind I was in. I kept my gaze forward. After spotting an altercation about to begin in the distance we decided to head back in the dome. I was ready to go back in. My heart was no longer racing. I had finally calmed. I knew I had to keep myself resilient.

We got back to our floor seats next to my grandmother and plopped down. The seeming long walk lasted only moments but with the lack of food, water, and an excess heat it felt more like hours. I sipped on a little bit of the water that was left in the bottle I had since that morning and decided to close my eyes for a little. It wasn't if I really had a choice. The heat was keeping me from doing much of anything else. It was either sleep or have continuous reminders of the awful smells of rotten food in the freezers and imprisonment in the largest enclosed arena in the world swimming around in my head. I closed my eyes for a few moments of sleep.

Hours later, I awoke to two National Guards men shinning flashlights in my eyes. I couldn't clearly make out their faces as the light blinded me. I squinted and placed my hand up to block the light from further interrupting my vision.

"You all as well! Out! Let's go!" One screamed using his flashlight to point in an unclarified direction. I was confused. I didn't know what "out" they were referring to. We snapped out of our sleepy daze and picked up everything that belonged to us, excluding the trash, as the guards continued to direct traffic. We didn't know which way to go or where we would end up. I saw a horde of people who looked just as we did start charging for the exit ramp. We decided to follow suit. My grandfather was right behind me and my grandmother behind him attempting to secure the lose pages and piece of paper tucked in her old Bible as usual. I decided to slow my pace to assist with them keeping up.

I finally realized where we were being herded off to. They were pushing everyone outside of the dome, through the same doors I met Hook Man. Seeing all of these bodies being shuffled towards the exit now reminds me of a book by John Boyne, *The Boy in the Striped Pajamas*. The story told a time where 9-year-old Bruno living in Berlin during World War II accidently lost his life marching into a gas chamber obviously not knowing what was about to happen. That final scene of his life mirrored what I felt was about to happen to my family and everyone around us. I just hoped we weren't being lead to our death.

The move was slow but no one complained or really questioned our forced travel. Finally, passing the doors to the exit, I looked back to see more of our kind following and looking frontward. Into the darkness showed hundreds of faces in the same predicament as myself. Huge spotlights were present but did not cure the dark entirely. We pressed ourselves into a corner of the crowd that was just the right size for three.

"They really getting us out of here! Thank you, Jesus! Ain't He good?" a lady with a faded blue head wrap shared with any ears that listened. My grandfather heard her words but still wanted to do his own investigating. He looked forward as far as he could to see what was going on up ahead. Not much could be explained from the back of the mass.

I looked up and noticed we were standing by a large clock near the Letter "C" indicating the section we were in. The clocks had halted. The little hands on them were frozen in place. Katrina had not only taken away our homes, our schools, but our time. The moments that were supposed to happen in New Orleans, the memories that would never occur, are countless. I was always in a rush to grow up, to be on my own, and to get somewhere but never realized how delegate life really is and how quickly time can be snatched from us. In that moment, I wanted to go backwards, but I couldn't. No one could.

As I pulled myself from my day dream, I saw a small woman hop up on a planter to add to her height. She began to scream into the crowd, "Hey! Them military people just told me they got 100 buses that hold 50 people a piece! We all going to Houston!" Some people cheered others booed as their families were in Austin, Dallas, and other places far from the reach of Houston. Most just accepted their fortune as they were too hungry, tired, and weak to be blissful or dissatisfied.

"Might as well settle in then," My grandfather started to find something for my grandmother and me to sit on, "If it's just a hundred buses, we gone be here for a while." He found us a box to break down and we took a seat avoiding the filth of the ground. Others soon decided to do the same trying to avoid the trash surrounding them. The smell made me think we were sitting in the middle of a landfill. The piles were high and the smell was smashing into our faces over and over again. One of the mates to a pair of worn out New Balance was sticking out of a nearby mountain of trash. I hoped that the smells were not from a dead body attached to the shoe in the pile. My grandfather decided that he would stand as it was a bit congested while my grandmother found a chair to sit in that had an injured leg but was still useable. It was so crowded people were literally on top of one another. Which explained the pair of long legs in black jeans laying in front of me; one nearly in my lap.

Lester. I had never met him before and didn't know him. I still don't. His mother called his name in order to grab something from the army green backpack he was wearing to give something to what seemed like a little brother. Those were only three of the thirty-eight family members that they claimed had stuffed themselves in the dome.

The one sitting neighboring me, Lester, couldn't have been more than fifteen or sixteen years old, the same as me. He barely had peach fuzz on his top lip. He had fair skin but there was a bit of white in the corner of his lip, clear signs of dehydration. He was wearing a green Iris jersey with gold trim and the name James on the back, the high school jersey of my least favorite NBA player of today.

We sat there, his leg on top of mine, until the line, rather crowd, started to inch towards our freedom. The sky was still an ocean of darkness when we found out that the buses weren't coming a hundred at a time. Word was passed back from the New Orleans Centre that it was more like four at once. Our seats constantly shifted as we moved a bit. My grandmother eventually found a thrown away storage bend to rest on to get out of the limping chair. The large luggage I owned my grandfather sat on in front of me. Still, Lester was sitting close. I tried to avoid eye contact by looking at my surroundings and playing with loose strings from my shirt.

There wasn't much to see outside but the heaps of rubbish of abandon luggage and children's toys. Some people were in dark spots outside of the beaming lights and I could not make out their faces. A young white couple decided they needed a smoke. The woman's hair was long but greasy. She was wearing a black tank top and plaid shorts revealing her boney legs. The man, who wore a white t-shirt with a faded US flag on the front pulled out what seem to be a cigarette. The woman took it from him and put a flame to the small roll of shredded tobacco.

It wasn't long before the smoke from their cigarette tickled my nose and divulge its true identity; good old cannabis. The smell was not new to me. Walking the streets of New Orleans, you were lucky if weed was the only thing you smelled. After a couple puffs a piece, the adults surrounding us gave the couple a look to force them to put it out. The woman placed the remaining bud in her pocket. As one of the adults moved away satisfied they had paused their habit, they unblocked the huge loud light, the brightness hit me directly in my eyes forcing me to speak out loud.

"The light is too bright!" I turned my head to motion away from the glare and up went my hand to block it, the same as when I was woken up by the Guardsmen not long before. My grandparents did not respond to my words but they were not the ears that were listening.

Lester turned to a family member, "See now she's got pretty eyes..."

"Who?" the boy asked as he looked around confused.

"Her," Lester pointed to me with his gaze. His whispering skills were horrible, "They're like light brown. Something like that. Not like that girl up there you were talking about!"

"Man, whatever. That other girl had a booty. She ain't gone like you no way," his darker family member explained.

Lester whispered something to him before speaking to me, "Say Red. Aye Red? What's your name?"

I looked at the light skinned boy and his wingman with revolt. Just like every other boy I've encountered in New Orleans to think this was the best time to hit on someone. I smelled like 6 days of hell, my hair was pulled back into a small puffball, much like the one that once was on the back of socks as a trendy fashion, and we were surrounded by filth. Not to mentioned I was starving, thirsty, and exhausted. It was not the time and surely not the place.

I decided to remove myself from the situation by getting up and sitting with my grandmother. Lester's conversation partner, I could hear laughing at him and at my rejection to engage. I didn't look back much after that and soon, with the light of day peeking out, his family along with mine was lost in the crowd. I never saw him or his green jersey after that.

The morning dragged. Smiles were not easily found. No food or water was provided as we waited for hours, a lot of us hadn't eaten since the morning before. We were on our own. Boiling bodies were bumping against each other, smashing in to one another like sardines in a can. While the heat hadn't crawled to its peak for the day, we could fill it approaching.

When the sun finally reached its highest point, we could easily sense it. It pounded down on our heads and we could literally feel our scalps overheating as we picked up pieces of rubbish to hold over ourselves to block the rays. We had reached the front of the crowd and could see the steel barricades the NOPD would use during Mardi Gras season. On the other side of the gates was a handful of National Guardsmen and women with long riffles in their hands and pistols on their sides. They marched back and forth waiting and ready for something to happen. A couple large fans were present and pointing towards them to keep cool. A case of water not too far away was not in the direct effect of the sun but out of reach to the general public. The few children that were left in the wait rested in their car seats or on the chest of their sweating mothers. The heat slowly took the natural glow from their sprits.

Everything was motionless with the evacuees until a guard yelled into the crowd, "Okay let's try to do this in an orderly fashion now!" He dragged one of the barricades against the ground constructing an opening to the guard's pit and it seemed to all be happening in slow motion. The mob began to push into the exit in order to get on one of the buses heading out of the city. A heavy set African American woman even shoved a man behind her and screamed "MOVE!" in order to create some personal space between them. Another lost the hand grip of her daughter but they soon found each other after their cries were matched and one of our prison guards grabbed the little girl to hand her to her parent. Then it stopped. The movement stopped and the gate was closed.

People were filled with disappointment. A sweaty man screamed out how he was angry that the 1100 buses were not full like they were supposed to be. Another voice reassured him we would be gone soon but there were never a thousand buses out there to save us. The guards tried to calm the people left behind but it was not working for them.

One lady of our flock started to scream, ""Let us out! Let us out!" She threw her fist into the air. People all around us started to follow.

"Let! Us! Out!"
"Let! Us! Out!"
"Let! Us! Out!"
"Let! Us! Out!"

Even my grandmother started to shout, "Let us out!" Over and over she yelled. I looked back to see if my granddad was also engaging in the mob's angry motions. But he wasn't. He was standing there with his head down, he expressed he was dizzy and using me as a prop bent down on one knee. I tapped my grandmother to get her attention.

She turned around to see him thirsty and overheated, "Burnell! Oh my Lord! Burnell!"

He did not respond as his eyes were now closed. Another woman witnessed what was happening and yelled to the military guards, "He's dying out here! We dying out here!" Her words were going unheard. The crowd's mighty sound was too loud to hear her small voice. My grandmother's eyes began to water as I rushed to my grandfather's side. The love for that man was clearly on her face. She was not about to let him just die. She was close enough to one of the gates to catch the attention of a guard.

As the sound of the mob ceased, it was easy for Grandma Ludie to yell out and be heard, "He's hot! He's too hot! He needs water or something! He needs help!" The man in uniform took a quick glance towards where my grandmother was pointing. More people had begun to notice my grandfather's decrease in health and picked up items to fan him. The national guardsman followed by looking to his feet. A half drank Gatorade bottled with a warm red liquid inside laid at his combat boot. He bent over, moving his weapon out of his way, and picked it up to hand to my grandmother.

The only words he spoke, "Poor this on his head."

"What the hell is wrong with you? What am I supposed to do with that?" My grandmother slapped the bottle down out of his hand which was followed by him simply walking away undisturbed.

"Here you go ma'am," a dark skinned man in his late thirties near us waiting handed a new bottle of water to my grandmother to help. A silent "thank you" and "you're welcome" was exchanged right before my grandma twisted the plastic top. She forced water in his mouth and then I poured some over his head.

"Burnell! Don't you leave! Don't you leave!" She was afraid of him dying on her. He was one of the few things she had left. He could not die.

"I'm okay Ludie," He put up his hand to signal she could stop while his eyes remain closed.

A lady behind us gave him a towel to put over his head while others moved in a position to try to block some of the sun all while still fanning. He drank more of the water and slowly began to feel better. The sight of people helping people was amazing. We had to depend on ourselves as others were only going to hand over options that would only make the situation worst.

As we were getting Grandpa Burnell back to normal the crowd calmed. All was peaceful again until one man decided to argue with one of the uniformed personnel. The black man was enraged and tired of his situation. He, much like everyone around him, was angry.

"Get us out of here!" The man reached out to grab one of them as he spoke. Then the guard reacted by drawing a weapon and pointing it into the crowd. The mass in fear, began to run backwards. Women screamed and children were in shock. Men who were not even involved instantly put their hands in the air, a hood signal for "I have no weapons. Please don't shoot." A young woman snatched a car seat from the ground just in time to prevent her child from being trampled. People fell back on their hands. The crowd was filled with fear of the people who were supposedly there to protect us.

A man's voice yelled, "Put it down! Put the weapon down!" Even being a distance away I could see the fear in all of the guard's faces. My grandfather still on his knee knew nothing of what was happening but I did. I knew blood was about to be spilled right in front of me. My heart raced as my grandmother pulled me in close to her. The guns were pointing in a different direction than were my family and I stood but I knew this would not end well.

I closed my eyes as I gripped my grandmother's midsection and ask God to fix this. God, please don't let them shoot nobody. We don't need this. Please! If you can hear me! Please!

I opened my eyes and the weapon was no longer pointing into the crowd. People were confused and afraid but silent. The fear was disappearing but so was the trust.

# Chapter 18: Grandpa's Old Shoes

*"Give a girl the right shoes, and she can conquer the world."*

**-Marilyn Monroe**

I never really understood the church culture. I know maybe not all churches but the many I have attended do the same routine over and over and over again. Every Sunday it was one of three things: give us money for a building fund, just pray to God so he can make your problems go away, or homosexuality is wrong and you will go to hell. Of course there were the occasional sermons of the birth of Jesus during Christmas and his crucifixion during Easter. That building fund never seemed to get the church a new building. The prayers for my problems to go away never worked but I was use to that. The one that stuck out to me the most was homosexuality being a sin and it was best to keep my hands in my pockets.

My grandmother knew I would be in a relationship with a woman even before I did. When I was really young, so long ago I can't even recall an age, she would grab my face and look me in my eyes, "Baby, you either gonna marry a white man or somebody's daughter. I can see it all in you, now. You gone be a bull dagger." I had no idea what those words meant but she wasn't far off. I don't think she intended to hurt me when she said it but to warn me of what others may perceive. I guess a mother, or a grandmother, really does know their child.

Instincts of being in love with women first appeared when I was around seven. I was way more interested in Gina than Martin in his sitcom. Watching reruns of *In Living Color*, I still remember lusting over the Fly Girls even though I didn't know what those feelings were. Sneaking to watch one of the movies in my uncle's collection, The Player Club, I fell into a secret relationship with LisaRaye McCoy that she still knows nothing about.

My first experience with a girl was when I was about ten. It was nothing serious, merely holding hands and a kiss on the cheek, but to me it was the world because another girl had the same feelings I did. Soon, however, my predispositions to be near a pretty miss was hushed by the fears that God would strike me down. I hid who I was for years because I didn't know *what* I was.

I did have relationships with the opposite gender but something was always missing. Those interactions, however, seemed like someone was sending men in my direction from a temp agency. I knew in the back of my head they would never be there long because they were only there to fill a void.

None of the dealings with guys were really pleasant to begin with. In middle school, I remember a boy who was in a grade higher trying to force me to kiss him in the stairway. I was able to push him off of me but he always gave me the stank eye in between classes. I never liked the forcefulness of some men; thinking they could make me do whatever they pleased.

Then, I married a man, Luke who I was not in love with, when I was very young because my grandfather told me when I was growing up that it was the right thing to do. That in God's eyes, I needed to be married. It didn't last long as he did not love me either and was very abusive both mentally and physically.

I once thought I found what I was looking for with another guy years later, Craig. This was the one time I truly believed that maybe all men weren't half bad. Unlike most guys who were very determined, he was patient. He never pressured me for months in our relationship to do anything with him. He was quite the charmer and very good with words. He was the perfect man in my eyes. We spent most of our time together during the week and on most weekends doing the normal things couples do like watching movies, going to dinner, and bowling. He was very materialistic and always wanted the finer things in life.

We were together for a while, happy, and enjoying every moment we could together. Then I got pregnant. Things would never be the same after that. While I thought this was the best news ever and that he would be happy to be having another son, I was sadly mistaken. In the parking lot of a fast food restaurant while sitting in the car with him he would express that he can't really do this with me. I was so confused at what exactly it is he cannot do when everything between us seemed perfect, I wanted to know specifics. The words leaving his mouth after that caught me surprise. He informed me that he was with someone else, whom in which a few weeks later after playing detective, I found out was his wife. She had been his wife for years! I couldn't believe that this was actually happening to me. There were no signs at all that he was capable of being with anyone else. I mean how could he, considering the amount of time we spent together and the fact that he lived alone. I was at a complete loss for words.

He didn't want me to have this child. He didn't want me. He waited it out, so I thought, to make himself seem like the perfect gentlemen. But it was all a lie. Against his wishes I still had my son, even if it meant I'd have to do it all alone. To be honest, for a split second, I even thought that maybe he would change his mind once the baby was here. It never happened. He wasn't there for any of it, he made the choice to give all his parental rights away, and he never even told his family he had another child in this world. I was going to have to do this alone. My first child. What should have been one of the most exciting times in a first-time mom's life, was no where near what I imagined it would be like. He took that moment.

Years passed by without any sign of him wanting to be a father to my son until I again decided I should try to force a bond with him for the sake of my child. I would beg him to do things like come see him or at least call and FaceTime him every now and then just so my son knows he exist. That would last only a few weeks, if that, before he would start ignoring me again. I got so furious at one point about the rejection he had towards my son, like I made him by myself, that I warned him he had to do something soon or I was going to personally go tell his family that he has another kid. What he did in regards to my promised threat? He chose to send money instead, every two weeks, to keep my silence and his secret of another child from being known. While I accepted this for a while, I ended up a short time after telling him to cease all payments as I knew that it takes more than a few deposits of cash to be a father.

I opted out of that life for my son because to me he deserved more. He didn't need any money, he needed the person who helped create him to be there. He was a boy who would need his father's time, love, and affection. I honestly believe I tried so hard and made a fool of myself mostly because I was in love with the idea of being a normal family not even because I wanted him anymore. I mean, how could I possibly want to be with someone who could lead me on in the way that he did and verbalize that I should get rid of the beautiful life growing inside of me?

I had been so brained washed by society that I wasn't being true to myself. To the world it is better to be a cookie cut version of the American dream, having a mother and father with a white fence and a golden retriever than to be truly happy. Being different is being wrong. I was willing to avoid being who I was with a man even though he treated me, and all of the other women he had, like disposable silverware. He showed me that I was not built for the destruction a guy could cause but also showed me I can't let what other people believe as being the right way of living push me to do something or be with someone that I really shouldn't. You would think I would be done with guys completely after that but I was never the type to make others pay for what my past had done. I did continue to casually date a few times later down the line, even met a decent guy and got into another committed relationship, but I was never truly satisfied and opted to be single again. This time for a long while so that I could truly focus on myself and my growing son.

Thinking back, I could never even complete the dream of me being with any man. I never visualized a man holding my hand on my death bed or us rocking on our porch with glasses of lemonade at 72. Every time I looked to my side to see who was holding my hand in my fantasy, the hand would not be attached to that of a gentleman. I tried so hard with them to make it work because I thought that was what I was supposed to do. I was supposed to be with a man. My heart was just never fully committed and with every connection with a dude I had, it was clear he would never be able to make me happy. Neither of us could ever give what the other required. I felt I was myself the most when with a she rather than a he.

My grandfather and uncle knew nothing of my feelings towards the same sex. I'm not sure how they would have taken the news back then knowing I was eyeballing Lisa Turtle from *Save By the Bell* and Hillary Banks from *Fresh Prince of Bel-Air*. I'm sure they would have had their opinions even though their behaviors never helped sway me to seriously consider being with a man for the rest of my life anyway. My uncle had his own playerish ways. I can remember sneaking into his room, stealing condoms, and filling them with water thinking he would never miss them as he had so many. The look on my grandmother's face when I asked her why all my water balloons had a greasy substance on the outside of them could kill.

Grandpa Burnell was not innocent. Even though the relationship between him and my grandmother was a bit bizarre, he still doesn't get a pass. They once were in love, or some variation of it, as they had my uncle together. My mother Yolanda and Aunt Tressa came before my grandfather to a man who would beat my grandmother during their time together. As the story has it, my grandpa saved Grandma Ludie from the relationship and then ran off towards Los Angeles, but not before relieving their current job of a few hundred dollars to get them through the journey from Texas.

My grandfather never was a saint and it didn't help the situation that he wasn't half bad looking either. He attracted a lot of attention from the ladies in New Orleans, much like his son, and those ladies were a lot younger than my grandmom. Worst part, my grandmother knew it. She found out about one of the the women who my grandfather called Country but she was only one of the many he had.

Grandma Ludie would ask me if I had anything on my grandfather or if I saw anything fishy happening when she wasn't around. While he was near a lot of women, I honestly didn't know what to tell her. When she asked about numbers she would find in his pants pockets or rumors from the store he worked he would reply only with, "Woman! All them women are my friends! Now calm the hell down!" She wouldn't really believe it I know, but she would stay. For years, she put up with the possibility of her not being the only women in my grandfather's life. My grandma was tired. I'm not really sure which event in her life with her partner changed her, but my grandmother decided to find a friend of her own. I guess my grandfather ways finally drew her into the clutches of Satan and she no longer wanted to be that "holy woman" anymore.

I was too young to understand the words my grandmother told me at the time, but it didn't take long for it to seep in, "Baby, know this!" She began rushing me towards the entrance of the church as we were already late. "If you want a good wholesome man, get one in the church! Those are the ones you can trust!"

She pushed the wooden doors of the tiny religious room at Little Mount Olive Missionary Baptist Church open for us to make way to our seats. I could hear the bang of the drums and tambourines bouncing against hands across the ministry. Women were singing along to the Christian music. A couple of little girls in the back row were opening a peppermint to keep them satisfied through service. As we made our way, I looked up to my grandmother to see her smiling towards the front in the direction of the piano player who held double roles being the director for the music ministry as well. I had never seen her smile so bright. Her eyes were as big as billiard balls. I think what I was witnessing was love.

It just happened. All out of the blue my grandmother had an adult crush on the aristocrat who played the piano, Mr. Wayne. He would have never been invited to be on the cover of a GQ magazine, but he was in the house of the Lord and he was a sweet man. I remember him being tall and slender. His hair was bushy and thick. There were dimples that cornered his smile which was missing a couple teeth and his fingers were long, making it easy for him to show off his music talents on the church's keyboard. I remember him not having much of his own. When I say that, I mean he didn't have anything at all. He was recovering from a drug addiction and he was proud to sermonize it. While I was happy that my grandmother was smiling at every site of this man, I didn't really know what all of that was going to lead to. I knew he was a nice guy but was he trying to replace my grandfather?

Grandmom fell for him; hard and fast. She wanted to help him in any way she could. I think she was trying to help herself more than anything. She was in a loveless relationship and she wanted out, even if that meant being with a recovering addict from the local church while still living with my grandpa all under the same roof.

I got lucky in the fourth grade and got to be a Wilson Wolves cheerleader for my school. My uncle would fund my little obsession even though it didn't last a full season as children still teased me and I eventually wanted out. The events would happen on a few Saturdays, and while my grandparents never went to any of them, my overprotective grandma would be stationed right on the corner waiting for me to get off of the bus in front of my elementary school like clockwork. Others would point and laugh as they got to walk home alone if their moms didn't drive to pick them up.

Then there was that one Saturday things were different. I got off of the big yellow bus that brought us back from a cheerleading competition, that I didn't get to actually perform in, to find my grandmother was not there waiting on me with a bottle of water in one hand and her Bible in the other. *Where is she?* I thought to myself. I stood on the corner in my green and white cheerleading getup puzzled. I quickly got over it when one of the other cheerleaders said she would walk the four blocks with me home.

When we reached the steps of the coral colored house on Delachaise Street, my classmate smiled, waved good-bye and disappeared around the corner to Broad Street. I opened the stormed door and walked in. I knew someone was home. I could smell food coming from the kitchen and I heard the blasting of gospel music coming from inside. I walked through the small sunroom and into the living area. There sat, in my grandfather's favorite spot on the couch, in the same seat where he watched his thrift store bought TV, the piano player, Mr. Wayne.

"Hi Tyierra. How you doin'?" He smiled a toothless smile as I stood in the entranceway.

"Fine," I replied surely with a confused look, "Where's my grandma?" I asked in hopes he would point me to where my grandmother was hiding. I remember thinking he killed my grandmother and put her in a pot on the stove explaining why she couldn't walk me home. He was just waiting for me to come in so I could be next. That has to be the only reason why she didn't pick me up.

He pointed towards the smell, "She in the kitchen.

*I knew it! She's in the pot!* I never turned around but instead walked backwards to the entrance of my house so not to take my eyes off of him. Something didn't sit right. So I decided to take a seat outside on the steps, just to be safe. Not even two minutes later, my grandmother came outside and asked me if I was okay to which I bobbled my head yes. She told me not to leave the steps and she would be right inside.

"You sure?" I asked thinking Mr. Wayne was either holding her under gun point or it was a trick.

"Yea," she smiled, "it's okay. I will be right inside and the window is open. If you need me holler."

*Again, I am left unattended!* For a normal child it meant nothing but to me it was really odd. Everyone knew my grandmother was franticly overprotective of me and wouldn't let me check the mail unaccompanied let alone sit on the stoop. *What is going on here!*

My uncle pulled up in his hoary car about half an hour later. He called it an antique, and I called it junk. I don't remember what it was but I do remember it being sticky in the back seat and I hated the smell. The look on his face was unforgettable! He got out of his car, slammed the squeaky silver door and seemed to be just as confused as I was.There I was alone, in my cute little cheerleading outfit outside. He walked up to me to study the situation.

"What are you doing outside? Where is mamma?" Maybe he assumed I had done something. But it wasn't me this time. I didn't reply. He asked me again, "Tyierra, where is mamma?"

"She's in the house," I mumbled as I stared up at him.

He yanked the white screen door open looked back at me and walked in. Almost instantly, I heard the loud roars of two men coming from the open windows of our house. Soon to follow was my grandma's voice attempting to break things up. Next came the sound of heavy feet running across the hardwood floors towards the front door. The screen crashed into the side of the house as Mr. Wayne jumped down the stairs. The musician ran as fast as his feet could carry him. Right behind him was my uncle with his keys in his hand. He darted towards his car, forced the car to start up, and away he went in the direction of the uninvited guest. My grandmother came out of the house and began yelling for my uncle to have mercy.

My Uncle Juney stopped in the street and yelled back at my grandma, "You got this man in my daddy house? Eating food that my dad bought? I'm going to tell Pop!" Once again he was off like a bat out of hell towards my mom's unofficial boyfriend. I could see in the distance the raggedy classic car slowing down next to the guy, I am sure not saying any words that would be encouraging. Once he was done torturing Mr. Wayne, I could hear my uncle's tires cry as he sped off in the direction of my grandfather's job. Mr. Wayne voyaged in the opposite direction.

My grandmother quickly dragged me in the house. My heart was beating from my chest and I was a nervous mess. After sitting me on the couch, giving me a glass of water and telling me to not go back outside, she went into the kitchen, calmly. I invited myself into the kitchen minutes later. She stood over the pots just stirring them. I stood behind her far enough away to not be noticed as she just kept moving the big table spoon around in that rusty old pot. She walked over to the sink to get a fork. I couldn't see her face anymore. She sniffled a little bit.

"Are you okay?" I asked my grandmother trying not to upset her further.

"Yea baby, I'm fine. Are you hungry?" she turned back to me and I could see the trail of a tear left behind. She noticed me looking at her and she wiped her face to get rid of any evidence that she was brokenhearted. She gave me a plate of food and instructed me to sit on the floor and watch a little television. I did as I was told.

*BOOM!*

Again, stumping across the floor heading quickly in my direction. Only fifteen minutes after sitting to eat something, a more uncomfortable sound had entered the house. My grandmother heard the noise and she screamed from the kitchen for me to go into one of the bedrooms. Leaving my Saturday cartoons and my meal on the floor, seconds before I got to my room, I heard a crash and then my mother yell out. My grandfather's voice repeatedly screamed at her to shut up. I closed my door and laid down on my pillow. I didn't know how to feel. Was I angry with my grandmother for bringing another man into the house upsetting my grandfather or angry with my grandfather for hurting and being so mentally frustrating to my grandmother? I laid there and listened to the muffled sounds of an argument until I drifted to sleep. There was no more talk of Mr. Wayne that night.

About a month later, I was resting in my room staring at the ceiling wondering whatever it is little elementary school-aged girls wonder. My grandmother walked in and started speaking softly to me to ensure my grandfather couldn't hear the awful news she was about to tell me.

"Tyierra, Mr. Wayne is coming over here later tonight," she whispered as she looked around to make sure my grandfather had not snuck in behind her.

"Huh?" I looked to her confused. *What is grandma thinking?*

She put her finger over her lips to signal me to be silent about the situation. I laid back and continued my mind drifting.

It was after nine that night and I was sitting on my bedroom floor writing. It was pretty quiet. My grandmother was in her bedroom pacing. I remember hearing the floor boards creak as she moved back and forth attempting to get her thoughts together. I walked down the short hall to peak in on her. I could see it in her eyes that she was nervous. My grandfather got up from the couch and headed to the bathroom. I sprinted back into my space before he could see I had exited. My grandmother gasped as she thought he was coming to her room. She held her breath until the door of the bathroom was closed. He brought a book with him letting us know he would be in there for a while. I snuck off back to my room but could still hear my grandma and her nervous pace back and forth.

Then I heard the doorbell. Grandma Ludie jogged to our front entrance. I just stayed in the door way of my room curious to see who it could be although I knew the obvious.

My grandfather yelled out from the bathroom, "Who is that at the door?!" My grandmother couldn't answer because she was busy letting that person who rang the bell in and I just did not want to be the one to tell him. I just stood there grasping my doorknob in wait. "WHO IS THAT AT MY DOOR THIS LATE AT NIGHT?"

I was frozen with fear. This had nothing to do with me and that was clear but I was still covered in panic. I backed up some but still remained close enough to see this man who had cause a problem before, Mr. Wayne, enter my mom's bedroom wearing an enormous red t-shirt, battered blue jeans, and the most unattractive pair of tennis shoes I have ever seen. The door remained open but it still felt wrong just knowing he was in there.

My grandmother was all for helping people. She would give anyone the shirt off her back and the shoes off her feet and I mean that literally. I could hear faint whispers between the two of them. I even heard a few giggles like teenagers at a drive-in movie. Then, while my grandfather was still in the bathroom probably puzzled to why no one had answered him, my grandmother called me into her room.

"Baby," my grandmother looked at me, "Mr. Wayne busting right out of these shoes. He has a hole in one of them. Go in that hall closet and give me a pair of them shoes your grandfather don't wear no more. I think they wear the same size shoe."

*What is she thinking?* I don't think she was thinking at all! Even though I felt fear in my hands, I had to do what I was told. I walked out of her room, passed the bathroom where my grandfather was still sitting in wonder, and into the hall closet. There was a pair of brown old beaten up shoes that my grandfather hadn't worn in a very long time. I remember the day he spent the $4 on them at the second-hand store. While they weren't in the best condition, it was better than what Mr. Wayne had on already. I grabbed them and headed back over to Mr. Wayne and my grandmother, tip toeing so not to alert my grandfather. Mr. Wayne clutched the shoes and I walked toward the door to make my exit.

"Thanks baby girl!" Mr. Wayne smiled at me as he spoke loudly in order to ensure I heard his words of gratitude. He slipped on his gently used shoes. I am sure he knew I was uneasy about the situation. I turned and gave him a fake smile and continued to walk out.

"'Baby girl?' Who the hell is in my house callin' somebody baby girl?!" I still couldn't find no words to fill my grandfather's ears.

I was stuck in the fast approaching cross fire standing right in between my grandfather's voice and my grandmom's fear.

I glimpsed over my tiny shoulder to see my grandmother attempting to keep the church keyboard player from saying something that would explode the situation. As my grandfather continued to scream from his uncomfortable position, the two new love birds debated back and forth on whether or not things needed to be said. Finally, Mr. Wayne pushed my mother's pleads aside and addressed my grandfather.

"How you doin', Sir?" He spoke with a raspy deep voice, "I'm Wayne. I met Ms. Jones at church."

"I tell you what!" the pages of the book my grandfather had bought in the bathroom with him began to make rattling sounds behind the door "if you ain't gone by the time I'm out of here, there will be hell to pay!"

Mr. Wayne attempted to heed my grandfather's warning but my grandmother was not allowing it. I saw the concern on the face of Mr. Wayne. He did not plan on seeing what my grandpa had up his sleeve for men who messed with his woman. Wayne tirelessly tried to escape while Granny Ludie yelled out to my upset grandfather, "This is my house too and I can have any one of my friends over if I want to! You do! So I will too!"

"Just wait until I get the hell out of here! I will show you who house this is!"

My grandma's gentleman caller was confused. I am sure he was not completely aware of the situation between my grandparents but he surely did not arrive at our home with the intentions of being in some marital madness. Mr. Wayne finally broke free and zoomed pass my grandmother off to the front door, all still while wearing my grandfather's old brown shoes and leaving his once white tennis behind. My grandmother quickly followed as she yelled his name over and over but no reply came from the musician. He had decided that it was wrong for him to be there and it would be safer to just leave at this point. My grandfather finally surfaced from the restroom and ran after the two. His pants were not bulked and the zipper was still down. I could hear the air rushing from my grandfather's nostrils as he grew closer to my grandmother. I followed but kept my distance.

"Wayne! Wayne! Don't leave me! Please, don't leave me here!" My grandmother was nearly in tears. I'm not sure if she was afraid to be left alone with my grandfather because she feared what he was going to do to her or if she truly didn't want to be alone anymore.

My grandfather heard her cries for the mysterious man in red to return. It only fueled his anger. While my grandma continued to yell for all of our neighbors to hear, my grandfather rushed behind her and pulled her down by her dark brown hair hitting her face on the stairs she was standing on and chipping one of her teeth. As he continued by dragging her back into our house, blood began to stream from her mouth landing on each step.

Light cries fell from her lips as she tried to rip his hands from her long hair but it was of no use. He continued to drag her while she kicked and plead for help. I screamed at him to stop but it was of no use. Even my shrieks for help were useless. No one came.

He finally got her through the door slammed it and relentlessly went on with pulling her across the floor into the living room. He took her body and threw it against the foot of the sofa. He turned to me as my shouts distracted him and told me to get in my room. I slowly walked away. I sat in my room with my back against the door hoping the sounds would stop. Low but still audible, I could hear my grandmother asking for Mr. Wayne to return. He was gone. Mr. Wayne was off and had disappeared into the hot New Orleans night.

"Girl, where are my damn shoes?!" I was sitting in front of the television when my grandfather came running to me from the hall closet. My grandmother was still sleeping off the night before hurting mentally and physically. I didn't get to see her the entire day but I could feel she was not whole. I will admit I was a little afraid that what happened to my grandmother would soon happen to me, "I know you were in there last night! Where are they?"

*Am I supposed to tell him where they were? Should I lie?* I decided that the truth would be my best bet at this point, "Mr. Wayne has them. She gave them to him because his were old and had holes in the bottoms," my head dropped. I did not like being put in the spot. I didn't want to lie but I didn't want to cause anymore issues. I was tied to my feeling of heartache.

The anger that came over my grandfather shielded him. He was a different person filled with disgust, irritation, and rage. When he spoke to me again, he was calm so not to scare me more than I already was.

"Where's this devil church that you and her go to so I can get my shit back?" he looked at me waiting on an answer.

I tried to give him directions on how to get there. Instead of going on his own, my grandfather requested I show him personally. He knew there would be a choir rehearsal and he wanted to make sure he got to him before he decided to run off again.

The walk wasn't long at all. The church was directly across the street from my school. As we got closer, we could hear the beautiful hums of music. The sounds of talent filled the air surrounding the house of worship but would soon be interrupted.

My grandfather swung opened the same doors his partner did the Sunday before and began to walk to the front of the sanctuary. Mr. Wayne's eyes filled with panic as he continued to play the ivories on the old piano. He didn't know what my grandfather looked like but he knew me and connected the two. The gifted choir, clueless, welcomed my grandpa and me in with open arms. Granddad Burnell stood in the isle slowly swaying to the melody as I hid my face behind him. They stopped singing in order to hear my grandfather speak. Mr. Wayne stopped playing the keys even though it was clear he didn't want to.

"How y'all doing tonight?" my grandfather gave them all a smile and they all replied with the normal responses of "blessed," "fine," and "happy to be here."

"Do y'all mind if I borrow your director for a minute?" No one denied his request. Mr. Wayne obviously was hoping the group would have a problem with him stepping out. He slipped from under the piano and began to walk out of the church behind my grandfather and I followed them both. His heart must have been racing not knowing what was going to happen next. He walked sluggishly in deep thought. The fear had to have been overwhelming.

"I will bring him right back," my grandfather assured the church goers.

Once outside, the big smile on my grandfather's face was gone. He turned around a few times to make sure no one was around to hear the wickedness of his spirit.

"Look man, I want my damn shoes!" my grandfather got real close to him when he spoke.

The man was wearing the shoes my grandfather was requesting at that very moment. He tried to plead with my grandfather, "So you gonna let me walk back up in this church with no shoes? Come on, that's not the ways of God."

"Ways of God? Don't preach to me! What's not of God is you coming in another man's house like you did. That's not 'the ways of God!' Now give me my damn shoes before I beat the shit out of you in front of this church!"

"Alright, man! You can have them," Wayne started gliding the shoes off his feet revealing his dingy purple socks. My grandfather continued to use foul language to convey to Mr. Wayne how worthless he was. With every word, I could see Mr. Wayne's manhood shrink up and vanish.

Once my grandfather had both shoes in his hand, he looked at the church's piano player in the eyes and said, "If I ever catch you near my house again I will break your neck!" Mr. Wayne guaranteed my father he understood, turned towards the doors to the church and walked in... shoeless.

When we got home, my grandfather opened the large garbage can that was in front of our house waiting for pick up and threw the shoes away. He then looked down at me and said, "I don't want those nasty ass shoes!"

# Chapter 19: One Last Ride

*"We are not retreating – we are advancing in another direction."*

**-Douglas MacArthur**

For about another hour, we were stuck out in the heat. Some of the people in the crowd stood while others sat waiting. It was not long before the lines began to move once more. We grabbed my grandpa and the heavy suitcase. I dragged it over a pile of trash while my grandmother assisted her life partner. We began our journey through the New Orleans Centre Mall viewing for the first and last time the huge skylight made of glass to the buses. Once passing through the massive mall that has now been turned into a VIP area for sporting events after Katrina's flood waters destroyed it, a uniformed man pointed me in the direction of one of the buses that was already filling up.

In order to get to the steps of our means of transportation out of NOLA, we had to step over some of what was left of the storm that was flowing down the normally busy road. I handed my large bag over to a man stacking things under the bus. As I moved to make my final steps on to the ride, the world slowed. I looked down the street to other buses and saw an old woman and young children making their last paces as I was without hesitation. Guardsmen were pointing people in the direction of the right locations to move. I inhaled a final dirty sniff as fumes continued to fill the air. The odor was enraged by the heat that had soaked into the sidewalks and the street.

I then found three seats close to the front of our ride to freedom. The cool air hit us all and at that moment I felt like royalty. Only queens would get this kind of treatment. I sat down near the window. My grandfather next to me, I could visually see his health improving. I took a deep breath. It felt like it was over. It wouldn't be long after our departure that it would be over for everyone. Fox news would soon report that the last person over the threshold of the dome was an elderly man dawning a Houston Rockets ball cap. He too was on his way to freedom. He had made it through the storm of Katrina and the dome.

Not all of the citizens of the Crescent City were as blessed. Two NOPD officers took their lives because of the negative effects from Katrina. The first to pass was Officer Lawrence Celestine allegedly by a self-inflicted gunshot. The case however, was put under investigation. The second life to be lost was Sergeant Paul Accardo, a media spokesman for the department, and his life too lost to a self-inflicted gunshot wound while sitting in a squad car.

More lives were taken in the storm, many that could have been avoided. Thirty-five patients in a St. Bernard Parish, husband-and-wife-owned nursing home died in floods when they were not evacuated. Unfortunately, the couple was found not guilty of their crimes. The city had lost more than could be counted. Not only were the streets still submerged but so were our hearts.

Once I was comfortable in my seat, I gazed out of the window and observed all the damage that was surrounding us. Glass was knocked out the side of buildings, trees in places there were not welcomed, and all of us on that bus were the only life that could be seen as far as I could tell. It was horrifying to feel this alone in the world.

The bus was soon set into motion. It felt as if we hadn't moved but mere inches before my throat started to dry and my eyes began to water. The only home I had ever loved was almost in the rearview mirror. I felt lost and afraid. I had always dreamed to travel around the world but I never thought I would actually leave. While I had been on a three-day Greyhound bus ride to Oakland, California to visit my aunt once, there were no family vacations for me. Spring break and summer vacation consisted of me staying on Orleans Parish soil stocking shelves at my grandpa's place of work. I wanted to travel the world but deep down in my soul I knew my future only had me being no greater than the city limits. Most people I knew who went away from New Orleans and its immediate outskirts came right back. It was, and still is, as if there really was a voodoo spell on the citizens. No matter where they tried to go in life, something always lugged them right back. New Orleans is where all of us felt safe.

We started our journey getting further away from the Superdome and while observing the city, it was nothing as I remembered a few days before. The silence was unreal. The streets were empty and there were no signs of life ever being there outside of the structures that were sitting empty. For it to be a weekend there was not one sign of a saxophone, tourist in the last days of summer, or people making their way to Canal Street for a little bit of shopping. There were no other moving cars or kids at play. It felt as we were the only ones left. It was scary to see nothing, to feel nothing, to hear nothing.

A raspy male voice behind us yelled to the driver, "Where we going, sir?"

The driver held on to his massive wheel as he bounced tackling a curve, "Texas. We all going to Texas."

It was a long ride to our destination. It was mostly quiet and the passengers barely moved. I was stuck only with my internal thoughts. I was thankful that my being trapped in my head this time came with a cool atmosphere around me. I thought about my uncle again, then every face in my school. My mind went to all of those people who I didn't know who had lost there lives.

*What are their families going to do? I wouldn't be able to make it without my grandparents.*

I looked over to my grandmother who was fast asleep, head bobbing with the motion of the fast moving bus. Her mouth was slightly opened and her Bible was gripped in her hands. My grandfather's head was tucked in his chest like a nesting bird. I was afraid for a moment he wasn't with us anymore until in the middle of his sleep he decided to scratch his nose. I smiled at them both. While they had given me hell at every turn, I knew I was not ready for them to leave. I knew I wouldn't be able to survive knowing the storm took the only family I had ever known.

For some of the city that hope was not there anymore. The world got to see the real break down of the birthplace of jazz when the image of Elvia "Vera" Smith's makeshift tomb made of bricks and a white sheet was broadcasted. The words "Here lies Vera. God help us" was spray painted with a cross and flashed across TV screens. Her remains laid on the street for four days before neighbors felt it only right to cover her.

Ethel Freeman, 91-year-old victim of Katrina was buried two months after her death. Her son, Herbert, after watching over her body for days being trapped in the Convention Center was ordered to leave her body and board a bus. In the days before her passing, she called out for help from a doctor and nurses, but there were none. They were on their own. Photos of Ms. Freeman's lifeless body were a dejected representation of just how slow response from our own government effected our people.

August Blanchard months later would come back to New Orleans and drive pass a small house in the Lower Ninth Ward where his grandmother lived. He didn't want to go in with fear that he would find her after being missing since the storm. An uncle would soon pass on the word that he indeed found her body under a sofa covered in mold near a teddy bear and a red blanket on February 25$^{th}$ 2006; nearly six months after Katrina.

So many others were overlooked in initial searches of houses throughout the city. Photos all over the internet now will have you believe that every house was searched as they showed a giant "X" on the exterior walls of homes and businesses. Each section of the mark had a different meaning. The top quadrant showed the date of the search. The left was the initials of the squad who conducted the hunt while the right was to show if there were any hazards noticed in the home such as "GL" for gas leaks. The final section, the bottom quadrant, noted any persons found, dead or alive. The process was criticized as some houses had the bright "X" on the front of the building but the doors were still locked signaling no one had entered. That left many to go back home to find loved ones in a situation they should never have had to.

I was blessed. To have made it out and to have made it with both my grandparents, I knew I was spared. I stared out the window and watched as the road ran under our wheels. I could only pray that the parts of my small family that were not sitting next to me were alive and safe. I closed my eyes and drifted away in to a comfortable sleep.

I was awaken by the doors opening in the parking lot of a Salvation Army later that night. All of the riders grabbed the few things they had left and exited the bus. We began walking to the front entrance. I watched as all of the riders looked around silently trying to figure out what part of Texas we had arrived.

"How you doing? Where are we?" my grandfather asked an officer who was holding the door for us to enter.

"Arlington, Texas sir," he replied as he smiled.

More cool air danced across our skin. We walked down a hall to find clothes and shoes were lined up against the wall for us to change into. But first we had to take a shower. We continued towards the main bedding

261

room that doubled as a basketball court in our absence. Beds filled the court from wall to wall. Others effected by the storm had already arrived and were settling in to their home away from the dome. Warm blankets and soft pillows sat waiting for us on three beds that were located against the home side of the basketball court.

The angels of Arlington provided us with soap and towels to take one of the best showers of our lives. I brushed my teeth and stared into the mirror while others moved around in the background. I hadn't looked at myself in days. I almost had forgotten what I actually looked like. But there I was. Tall, nappy headed, light skinned, and alive. Still alive because I had survived.

After leaving the shower my grandmother escorted me to a room where I could see a TV sitting on a wooden stand. Other children and parents were in the same space gazing at the screen. Sound from overhead was a video of New Orleans rescues of people stuck on roof tops filled the room. Every channel covered a different angle of distraction of our home.

"Where is my son?" My grandmother asked to any ear that was listening not expecting a response.

I looked to her and stared into her dim eyes, "We gonna find him. He's not in that. He's okay." As I grabbed her hand to ensure her everything would be better soon she nodded her head in agreement. I hoped that I was not providing her with false faith. She was feeling the same pains that so many others mothers and fathers were feeling in that same moment. They could not find their children and there was nothing they could do but sit in the room and listen to the news.

In that room is where I first heard the words from Kanye West. *A Concert for Hurricane Relief* to assist those effected by Hurricane Katrina had been put together on September 2$^{nd}$ and was being talked about in our full court room filled with Katrina Survivors.

I can remember the other adults talking around the moments Mr. West and Mike Myers, a comedian, got in front of a camera. West had made the decision to not read off of a teleprompter but instead add his own wording. That he did. In the middle of a live broadcast he said it:

"George Bush doesn't care about black people."

Hearing his words and knowing he had said that to the whole world made my mouth fall to my palm. His honest personality was being just that; honest. He said what everyone with a face like mine and from neighborhoods the same as ours was thinking. If it was anywhere else, for anyone else, it would have been different.

Each president I've been able to follow has carried their challenges and have brought reason for me not to trust them, some more than others. That is everyone outside of President Obama. Call me bias if you want but I can promise you it is not because he is black. It is because of the changes he made for not just people of color but every race, each gender, and all sexual orientations. Some say there were no changes suitcase in the other. My grandmother looked back to see I wasn't moving. She motioned toward me slowly.

"Tyierra, it's okay. This is almost over. We got one last ride. Just one more," Her smile and huge bubbly cheeks dragged a small smirk from me before she took my ticket to hold and grabbed my hand.

I sat down in my seat after loading my bag underneath. All of the memories of what had happened in the last few weeks seemed to use the glass bus window as a projection screen. From McMain, to Shandrika, and Terrian. Then visions of the posters I had badly tapped to my wall in my shared room in East New Orleans and the mess I had on the bed before leaving. I started to think of all the sights, sounds, and smells during my stay in the Superdome and how I almost lost myself. I remembered almost losing my grandfather and the crazy Hook Man will never be a distant recollection. But we made it. Katrina had not won.

As I fiddled with the dog chain with the engraved script, I focused my thoughts to a more positive place. *This is it. We got one last ride. Just one more.*

# Cover Copyright Notice

# Source Notes

"'Camp Greyhound' Home to 220 Looting Suspects." *The Washington Times*, The Washington Times, 9 Sept. 2005, www.washingtontimes.com/news/2005/sep/9/20050909-122226-7515r/.

Dewan, Shaila. "In Attics and Rubble, More Bodies and Questions." *The New York Times*, The New York Times, 11 Apr. 2006, www.nytimes.com/2006/04/11/us/nationalspecial/11body.html.

Gold, Scott. "Trapped in the Superdome: Refuge Becomes a Hellhole." *The Seattle Times*, The Seattle Times Company, 1 Sept. 2005, www.seattletimes.com/nation-world/trapped-in-the-superdome-refuge-becomes-a-hellhole/.

Holthaus, Eric. "The Most Dire Weather Forecast Ever Issued ." *Slate Magazine*, Slate, 28 Aug. 2015, www.slate.com/blogs/the_slatest/2015/08/28/hurricane_katrina_weather_forecast_robert_ricks_urgent_warning_changed_the.html.

"How One Couple's Desire to Rebuild New Orleans Nearly Tore Them Apart." *USA Today*, Gannett Satellite Information Network, 28 Aug. 2015, ftw.usatoday.com/2015/08/how-one-couples-desire-to-rebuild-new-orleans-nearly-tore-them-apart%C2%A0.

"Hurricane Katrina Statistics Fast Facts." *CNN*, Cable News Network, 28 Aug. 2017, www.cnn.com/2013/08/23/us/hurricane-katrina-statistics-fast-facts/index.html.

Jenkins, Sally. "By Hook or by Crook, Surviving Storm." *The Washington Post*, WP Company, 19 Sept. 2005, www.washingtonpost.com/wp-dyn/content/article/2005/09/18/AR2005091801397.html.

"New Orleans Police Ordered to Halt Looting." *USA Today*, Gannett Satellite Information Network, 31 Aug. 2005, usatoday30.usatoday.com/news/nation/2005-08-31-looting_x.htm.

Reeves, Jay. "Ten Years Later, Woman's Death Still Haunts New Orleans Neighborhood Struck by Hurricane Katrina." *Orange County Register*, Orange County Register, 20

Aug. 2015, www.ocregister.com/2015/08/20/ten-years-later-womans-death-still-haunts-new-orleans-neighborhood-struck-by-hurricane-katrina/%C2%A0.

"Refuge of Last Resort: Five Days inside the Superdome for Hurricane Katrina." *USA Today*, Gannett Satellite Information Network, 8 Oct. 2017, ftw.usatoday.com/2015/08/refuge-of-last-resort-five-days-inside-the-superdome-for-hurricane-katrina%C2%A0.

Rushton, Compiled by Christine. "Timeline: Hurricane Katrina and the Aftermath." *USA Today*, Gannett Satellite Information Network, 28 Aug. 2015, www.usatoday.com/story/news/nation/2015/08/24/timeline-hurricane-katrina-and-aftermath/32003013.

Shankman, Sabrina, et al. "After Katrina, Cops Given OK to Shoot Looters." *CBS News*, CBS Interactive, 25 Aug. 2010, www.cbsnews.com/news/after-katrina-cops-given-ok-to-shoot-looters/.

Terry, Josh. "10 Years Ago Today, Kanye West Said, 'George Bush Doesn't Care about Black People'." *RedEye Chicago*, 2 Sept. 2015, www.chicagotribune.com/redeye/redeye-kanye-west-katrina-telethon-george-bush-black-people-20150902-htmlstory.html.

"Tyler Perry Biography." *Biography.com*, A&E Networks Television, 8 Sept. 2017, www.biography.com/people/tyler-perry-361274%C2%A0.

WWL Radio. "WWL Radio Interview New Orleans Mayor Ray Nagin : Free Download, Borrow, and Streaming." *Internet Archive*, The Library Shelf, 4 Sept. 2005, archive.org/details/WWL_Radio_Interview_New_Orleans_Mayor_Ray_Nagin_.

Made in the USA
Coppell, TX
12 December 2022

89080769R00157